MW00715509

The Lies I Once
BELIEVED,
the Truth I Now
LIVE

Love,
Baba + Gido

Dianne M. Coonan
(my friend)

THE LIES I ONCE BELIEVED, THE TRUTH I NOW LIVE
Copyright © 2019 by Dianne M. Coonan

Scripture quotations marked (NKJV) taken from the New King James Version®. Copyright © 1982 by Thomas Nelson. Used by permission. All rights reserved. Scripture quotations taken from the New American Standard Bible® (NASB), Copyright © 1960, 1962, 1963, 1968, 1971, 1972, 1973, 1975, 1977, 1995 by The Lockman Foundation. Used by permission. www.Lockman.org. Scripture quotations taken from the Amplified® Bible (AMPC), Copyright © 1954, 1958, 1962, 1964, 1965, 1987 by The Lockman Foundation. Used by permission. www. Lockman.org. Scripture quotations marked MSG are taken from THE MESSAGE, copyright © 1993, 1994, 1995, 1996, 2000, 2001, 2002 by Eugene H. Peterson. Used by permission of NavPress. All rights reserved. Represented by Tyndale House Publishers, Inc.

Printed in Canada

Print ISBN: 978-1-4866-1845-3

Word Alive Press
119 De Baets Street, Winnipeg, MB R2J 3R9
www.wordalivepress.ca

Cataloguing in Publication may be obtained through Library and Archives Canada

I dedicate this book to Harvey, my husband. I thank God for the man he gave me as a helpmate. He is a kind, gentle, loving, forgiving, giving, and faithful man. Thank you for never giving up on me, on us.

Contents

Contents

Acknowledgements

Thank you to every person that has crossed my path and has been part of my life. You have influenced me along my life journey. Special thanks to the many followers of Christ who prayed, encouraged, challenged, and loved me. It is almost impossible to thank everyone who helped make this book possible, but I would like each of you to know how grateful I am and thankful for your help.

Thank you to the Father, who called me, encouraged me, and set me free to write by His guidance and love. All glory and praise to Him.

Introduction

How can a person know the truth, yet live lies? You may know the truth, but because of your woundedness or lack of a full revelation of the truth, you choose to listen to the lies of the enemy or the lies you tell yourself.

For me, that was easy. I knew Christianity taught that God loves you, that He forgives you and cares about you, that He's always there and that He is God. But my wounded heart determined my reactions, inner dialogue, and how I lived life. I was that person who learned something yet struggled terribly with her inner thoughts.

Through the healing process, the Father pursued me, continually loving me and encouraging me to walk in love and receive His love, forgiveness, approval, counsel, and caring heart so that I could walk in my identity as the person He created, not the person I or others said I should be.

Throughout this book, I would like to challenge you to look at your heart and ask yourself these questions: "Am I living loved by God? Am I living in the forgiveness of God? Am I living out of others' approval or God's approval? Am I being the person the Father created me to be, living in my true identity?"

It's amazing to sit back and realize that I actually believed in my intellect that I was loved, forgiven, and had approval but my heart dictated otherwise. I tormented myself with lies that most definitely did not fit the truths my intellect believed.

My life became a journey of being transformed from *knowing* the truth to *living* the truth. The process and journey continue to this day. I have journeyed toward believing the truth not only in my head but in my heart and my spirit. I could only live the truth as I allowed the Father to heal my wounded heart and distorted thinking.

Whatever your reason for reading this book, my desire is that as you journey with me through its chapters, you will be encouraged to ask yourself, "What does my heart believe?"

Throughout the book, I will sometimes reveal examples from my own life. Other times I'll skip personal examples in order to focus on the healing aspect, so as not to expose people in my life. I would not want to hurt, offend, or allow any kind of judgment to come on them.

Sometimes my hurt was a result of the accumulation of my own misconceptions, my own actions, and a combination of hurts that come from the world. My focus is on the healing, transforming power of our Lord, and to show how a heart can be changed with a greater infilling of His love along the journey.

I grew up in small towns in Alberta, being raised by a mom and dad in a family of three children. We always had good meals, clean clothes, and a safe place to live. We attended church every Sunday, were surrounded by extended family, and had all our physical needs met. I loved school and did well in it. I was a good student, played sports, participated in the school band, and had lots of friends.

Looking at me from the outside, it seemed like life was great. I got married to a wonderful, loving man and we had children, attended church, had family living close by, and lived with very little frustration or conflict. One could say that life was good.

In this good life, though, my inner dialogue tormented me. I questioned most of my thoughts and actions, asking all the whys, how comes, and what ifs. I accused myself of not being acceptable and not performing satisfactorily.

Being set free from my inner dialogue was a process. As my wounded broken spirit was healed, my mind was freed as well.

In Luke 4:18–19, Jesus quotes Isaiah in announcing that He has come to set the brokenhearted free:

> *The Spirit of the Lord is upon Me, because He has anointed Me to preach the gospel to the poor; He has sent Me to heal the brokenhearted, to proclaim liberty to the captives and recovery of sight to the blind, to set at liberty those who are oppressed; to proclaim the acceptable year of the Lord.*
>
> —Luke 4:18–19, NKJV

> *The Spirit of the Lord God is upon Me, because the Lord has anointed Me to preach good tidings to the poor; He has sent Me to heal the brokenhearted, to proclaim liberty to the captives, and the opening of the prison to those who are bound; to proclaim the acceptable year of the Lord, and the day of vengeance of our God; to comfort all who mourn, to console those who mourn in Zion, to give them beauty for ashes, the oil of joy for mourning, the garment of praise for the spirit of heaviness; that they may be called trees of righteousness, the planting of the Lord, that He may be glorified.*
>
> —Isaiah 61:1–3, NKJV

Over the years, I've had people give me many scriptures, and this is one the scriptures that I remember and keep close to my heart. Christ was there to heal my woundedness. I knew He would help me.

Throughout the process of my wounded heart being healed and set free, I learned the Word of God and received revelation. I yielded and surrendered to the healing and revelation of the Holy Spirit. I allowed the love of the Father to touch me. I spent time in fellowship and prayer with the Father and submitted to the body of Christ, His people, allowing them to speak and minister into my life.

As a young child of two, I knew that Jesus existed, but I didn't know the truth of the Word. I loved Jesus, and my world changed when I gave my life to the Lord. I had faith to believe for others and wanted everyone to know Jesus. I attended Bible studies to learn the Word. I experienced physical, emotional, and spiritual healing in my life. In my deep desire to understand healing, I attended healing classes and studied online.

Yet through everything I experienced, I was often bombarded with thoughts which I now call lies of the enemy. This is the area of my life that I've chosen to write about. Through revelation in my heart, through the Holy Spirit, I have been set free from having a tormented mind. God is so good, even though it had become normal to fight lies in my head; God would still touch me and teach me. The Word still spoke to me. I learned about the occult, about how Jesus walked on the Earth, and about His Kingdom. There was so much to learn, and the Word is full of new revelations.

Like so many Christians, I have experienced the Father's touch on my life. Because I experienced the Father in this way, I never quit pursuing Him and He never gave up on me. I experienced miracles of protection while driving; I knew it was only by the hand of God that I did not get into accidents. I have been awoken in the night to pray for my son, only to have him call a half-hour later telling my husband and I that he was in an accident. I have so many stories of God helping my family and being there for us.

My faith has allowed me to trust God for the impossible. The medical field informed me that I would never have children, yet I feel so blessed that the Lord gave me three sons. I chose to look for the Father working in my life, to see His touches which I call miracles.

Yet I also had unanswered prayer, hurt, and pain in my life. Somehow, in the core of my being, I realized it is necessary for me to stay close to the Lord.

I call it a great testimony of revelation in my life when His Word speaks to me, teaches me, and helps me. Faith has been a constant in my life. Sometimes my faith was greater, and it seemed easier to believe and pray. Other times I needed to have the body of Christ help me. We need one another. I don't know where I would be without faith.

Come along on this journey with me. I pray that what I have learned and experienced in my journey of life will somehow touch your life and help you walk closer to the Father, the Son, and the Holy Spirit.

My family hasn't had to walk through extremely difficult trials, but in going through life we have had disappointments, hurts, misunderstandings, grief, joy, love, pain, and anger. We've experienced all the ups and downs that go with life. I don't have all the answers, but the revelations I've been given have helped me walk each day with the greater peace, love, and joy of Christ. As I am living on the Earth, I know that I won't have all the answers. I believe that we will continually receive new revelations and wisdom from the Lord, which changes us from glory to glory. But I do know that my mind isn't tormented anymore. It is free to live the truth, not lies.

My hope is that as you read this book, the questions and testimonies will encourage you to reflect on your thoughts and inner dialogue, on your words, actions, and deeds in life as they pertain to the truths in the Word of God. I pray that the Holy Spirit will show you areas in your life that He wants to touch with his healing and give you answers to your questions.

Opening your heart to the Holy Spirit can sometimes be scary and painful. I have learned not to fear allowing the Holy Spirit to touch the innermost parts of my heart, because each time I have opened my heart, I have been healed of an inner hurt, taught a new truth, or led deeper into repentance. The end result is that I have felt a greater freedom to be the person God created me to be and live with a peaceful mind.

The enemy is a liar, a thief, and a destroyer and I give all praise to the Father, Son, and Holy Spirit for exposing the lies and revealing the truth.

CHAPTER ONE

Starting the Journey of Truth

How do you read the Word of God?
How do you let it speak to you?
Is it just words or life-transforming revelations?
Do you read for information?
Does the Word touch your heart?

The Word of God can be all of these things to me. Sometimes, while reading the word, it seemed like I was just reading words. Other times I read for information to learn. Still other times I found the Word to be life-changing. The Word of God often speaks right to my heart, like the Father speaking to me directly and teaching me, touching my heart, which is my spirit, the core of my being. I call this revelation knowledge—it's transforming knowledge that renews the heart and mind.

> *And do not be conformed to this world, but be transformed by the renewing of your mind, that you may prove what is that good and acceptable and perfect will of God.*
> —Romans 12:2, NKJV

Over the years, this has become one of my favourite scriptures because it has been real to me. As I read the Bible,

I would ask the Holy Spirit, "What does the scripture really say?" I would ask, "Father, what do you want me to understand from this scripture?"

The Father answered in a variety of ways. I can remember listening to a speaker who said, "The Holy Spirit taught me on this scripture and I have been sensing there is someone here who has been asking the Father for understanding." I knew that was me, because he was answering the exact same question I had been asking. Sometimes my answer came in a book, and other times it came to me in the still, small voice in my heart.

Before starting to read scriptures, all I knew was how to follow all the rules. These are the rules I thought you had to follow if you wanted to live a good life, if you wanted God to be happy with you. It was easy to be religious and follow all the rules, but the hard part was trying to be the perfect person. The problem was that I could never measure up. I could never please everyone or do everything right. Most of all, I kept trying to be somebody I wasn't. I tried to be the perfect religious person, and it was never enough.

My mind had the misconception that if I read the Word and did my best to learn the truth, that would help me to be the person God had created me to be and I would be content. Learning the truth was wonderful, yet I found it wasn't enough just to know the truth in my head. Just knowing the truth in my head didn't allow me to live the truth in my heart.

I believed lies in my heart. For example, "You're no good. You're fat and ugly. You will never be good enough to be loved. You're too loud. You're too quiet. You're not fun enough. You always make mistakes and do the wrong thing. You try too hard. You say the wrong things. You should work more. You aren't a good representative of Christ." It went on and on.

I've realized that when you started believing a lie, you see everything through the eyes of that lie. Because I believed I was fat, ugly, and unwanted, I believed that those three things went together. When I went out, I would feel unwanted because my belief system. My thoughts would tell me that if I was thin and pretty, I would be wanted. There's no truth to that, but only the Father was able to reveal the ways in which my heart was perceiving the lie and not the truth.

I was very aware that when I felt uncomfortable, I told myself, "I'm fat and ugly and not good enough." My husband would tell me not to say that. I knew I shouldn't say those things, but I would just shrug it off. I thought that was who I was. There's an interesting story about how the Father revealed to me that I needed to be healed. The Father, in His great love and mercy, arranged circumstances in my life so that He could reveal to me that I needed healing.

While attending a retreat, one of the speakers spoke about how the Father wanted her to speak about the part of her heart that believed she was fat, ugly, and unwanted. Before the retreat, I had said, "Father, what is still left in my heart that I ought to deal with?" When the speaker began her talk, I fully related to what she was saying. I had a *wow moment*.

I thought to myself, *Father, you are speaking right to my heart. You want me to admit that my heart believes I am fat, ugly, and unwanted.*

My heart was wounded and needed ministry. As the speaker continued to share, I was amazed at how similar her story was to mine. In her inner dialogue, she had struggled with feeling fat, ugly, and unwanted. Afterward, I thanked the speaker for using those words, and she related to me how hard she had struggled with the Father to use the words *fat, ugly,* and *unwanted*—but she had known she had to speak them out.

3

The Father brought that speaker for me.[1]

I concluded that I had to forgive others, forgive myself, renounce the lie, and ask the Father to make known to me the first time I had felt unwanted. The Father's healing changed my tormented mind. I no longer worry. I'm no longer self-conscious. I no longer torment my mind with thoughts of being fat, ugly, and unwanted.

This story shows how easy it is for a lie to affect your life, without you being fully aware of it. I would never have said I was believing lies, because I wanted to live in the truth. I had been trying to live the truth, but my mind went elsewhere, bombarding me with thoughts of worthlessness, inadequacies, and doubt.

The Father would never say any of those things to me, but we have an enemy, satan, who is in this world bombarding us with negative lies. In the battle of life, satan uses whatever he can to lie, steal, and destroy our lives.

The thief does not come except to steal, and to kill, and to destroy. I have come that they may have life, and that they may have it more abundantly.

—John 10:10, NKJV

I started knowing about God the Father, Jesus His Son, and the Holy Spirit when I went to church as a child. I feel so blessed that I've had the revelation of the Trinity since childhood. I just believed! When someone asked me how I knew, I didn't really have an answer. I didn't need proof or scientific evidence.

---

1 I know her message spoke to others, too, but I felt this message was just for me.

Through the journey of life, I learned about God. My parents taught me what they knew, I attended catechism classes in school, I heard the readings in church, and I let the lyrics of worship songs penetrate my being. When I couldn't understand what was happening in church, I would read from the songbook and let the songs speak to me.

From the age of two, there was no question in my mind that I was going to follow Jesus. What I did question were the whys and how comes. I questioned God all the time when I talked to Him. At one point, I was just asking Him questions or asking Him to do things for me. If you would have asked me if I liked to pray, it wouldn't have taken me long to say "No." I never sat and recited the formal prayers. I didn't know that just talking to God was a form of prayer. I knew God was so real and that He was there watching over me.

But life happens—the joys, happiness, activities, hurts, disappointments, and misunderstandings. How do you deal with these? Where do you get the answers?

As we grow up, most of us get answers from the people around us. We listen to what is said and perceive what happens around us. Our minds get taught, but in my experience our hearts can get confused, even wounded. They can also be filled with joy and touched with love. The joy and love feels good and right. But I stuffed down all feelings that didn't feel like joy and love, choosing instead to live the way I thought the Father wanted me to live—happily. Sometimes I believed that the only emotion the Father wanted us to have was happiness.

I have now realized this is very dangerous, because there was a huge part of my heart I wouldn't let Jesus or even myself go into. Emotions are real, and they either get stuffed down or dealt with. Mine got stuffed down, and I wasn't going to go where those emotions were.

In your mind, you learn what you are taught. But attitudes, opinions, and emotions are formed in the heart through your experiences. Truth and lies are formed at the same time, causing confusion. God has created us with our own purpose and identity, but wounded and confused hearts don't allow us to be people God created us to be—especially when our hearts are stuffed with undealt with emotions.

Because being a good Christian was very important, I wanted to learn more about Jesus. I heard people talk about Him as though they knew Him. They talked about having a relationship with Jesus. I would roll my eyes and think, "Yeah, really." When I heard someone say, "The Lord told me that," I would think, *I really doubt it.* I would also think, *It sure would be nice to know that Jesus speaks to you, but how could that ever happen?* I believed the lie that Jesus doesn't speak to individual people.

> *"My sheep hear My voice, and I know them, and they follow Me.*
>
> —John 10:27, NKJV

One day as I was working in my garden, a voice spoke to me. I knew it was God. No one was going to tell me otherwise. I heard the words, "If you don't get your IUD removed, you will lose your baby."[2] I sometimes think back on this situation and marvel that I never questioned it. I just knew that God was speaking to me.

Taking the message very seriously, I went that day to the doctor to have the IUD removed. I then told God the Father, "If this is true, I will do everything I can to learn about you and follow you."

---

2   An IUD refers to an intrauterine device.

What the Lord had told me that day was true, and it saved my son's life. Nine months later, our beautiful son was born. Over the years, I've felt sad that I hadn't been fully informed that an IUD aborts an embryo and that it can take five to six days from the time of conception for an embryo to be implanted in the uterus. God, in His great love, saved our son and had mercy upon me. He did that for me and I was going to keep my promise.

This began my journey of learning the truth. God sent a minister to start a Bible study and I attended. That's where I began to learn about the Holy Spirit. Step by step, God introduced people into my life.

Who has God placed in your life to walk this journey? Where has the Father prompted and touched you with His love?

I started gathering with ladies for prayer and Bible study. One sweet elderly lady, whom I consider an evangelist, kept telling me that I needed to ask Jesus to be the Lord of my life, and that I needed to let the Holy Spirit work in my life.

One night, she had a vision of a group of sheep next to the shepherd and there was one little sheep running as fast it could to keep up with the herd. It just wanted to be close to the other sheep and the shepherd. I knew that was me.

That night, I told her that I would ask Jesus to be the Lord of my life and let the Holy Spirit work in me. Something changed for me that night. It was like my eyes were opened to see the things of the spiritual realm in a different way. The truth of the Word came alive to me. Reading the Word of God became so exciting and filled me with so much peace.

I had believed a lie for years, that reading the Bible was only allowed for certain people. If you weren't supposed to read the Bible, you wouldn't understand it. This was an untruth which had been passed down from generation to generation for years. The truth is that the Bible is for everyone to read and that the Word shows us the way. The Word of God is such a powerful gift, and it's given to us from God the Father to show us His love and character.

In my journey, I started to read and see the scriptures about the Word of God. What does the Bible really say about the Word?

> *Your word is a lamp to my feet and a light to my path.*
> —Psalm 119:105, AMPC

> *My son, keep my words; lay up within you my commandments [for use when needed] and treasure them… Bind them on your fingers; write them on the tablet of your heart.*
> —Proverbs 7:1, 3, AMPC

> *Jesus said to him, "I am the way, the truth, and the life. No one comes to the Father except through Me."*
> —John 14:6, NKJV

> *If you love Me, keep My commandments. And I will pray the Father, and He will give you another Helper, that He may abide with you forever—the Spirit of truth, whom the world cannot receive, because it neither sees Him nor knows Him; but you know Him, for He dwells with you and will be in you.*
> —John 14:15–17, NKJV

> *Jesus answered and said to him, "If anyone loves Me, he will keep My word… He who does not love Me does not keep My words; and the word which you hear is not Mine but the Father's who sent Me.*
> —John 14:23–24, NKJV

If you abide in Me, and My words abide in you…
—John 15:7, NKJV

Sanctify them by Your truth. Your word is truth.
—John 17:17, NKJV

Every Scripture is God-breathed (given by His inspiration) and profitable for instruction, for reproof and conviction of sin, for correction of error and discipline in obedience, [and] for training in righteousness (in holy living, in conformity to God's will in thought, purpose, and action)…
—2 Timothy 3:16, AMPC

Man shall not live and be upheld and sustained by bread alone, but by every word that comes forth from the mouth of God.
—Matthew 4:4, AMPC

So everyone who hears these words of Mine and acts upon them [obeying them] will be like a sensible (prudent, practical, wise) man who built his house upon the rock.
—Matthew 7:24, AMPC

The Bible is the Word of God and Jesus tells us to keep His Word and let it abide in us. How can you let the Word abide in you if you never read it?

I had learned much about God by hearing it. I knew the laws and traditions. I wanted to know Jesus—the truth, the life, and the way. I wanted the Holy Spirit the helper, the Spirit of truth, to be in my life. I needed help and I needed the truth. The real transformation in my life began when I started reading the Bible and allowing the Holy Spirit to be my helper.

The Bible is an amazing book. While reading it, sometimes I get information, but often I get a revelation and say to myself, *I've read this before, but today the Holy Spirit brought revelation, or today the Father spoke to me and spoke into my heart from the Word.*

I once had a friend ask me what I meant when I used the word revelation. Revelation means that a truth becomes real to me—not just words, not just laws. Revelation also shows me something I never understood before, so it brings understanding. Revelation sometimes comes in the form of a desire to learn and understand what the Word is saying. I must take heed to what is being said. Revelation may also come in the form of God's joy, love, or wisdom entering the depths of my heart. Revelation may come as conviction of wrong thinking or acting. Revelation is more than head knowledge; it touches your inner being, your heart.

> *Be anxious for nothing, but in everything by prayer and supplication, with thanksgiving, let your requests be made known to God; and the peace of God, which surpasses all understanding, will guard your hearts and minds through Christ Jesus.*
>
> —Philippians 4:6–7, NKJV

As I was reading these scriptures, which I have read many, many times, the Lord spoke to me and told me that I've missed part of the scripture. I give Him my prayers and requests and then guard my own heart, but He wanted me to know that if I gave Him my heart to be guarded, He would guard it. I don't have to guard my own heart. I don't have to be the protector of my own heart.

The following chapters will reveal some of the ways in which my heart and mind were transformed from believing a lie to believing the truth from the Word of God.

The Lie:
The Father doesn't speak to us, and the Bible
is only for certain people to read and tell us
what to do and what not to do.

The Truth:
The Father wants to speak and communicate with us.
His Word, the Bible, is one way of revealing Himself
to us, the revelation of His love and that we are
His sons and daughters.

My journey began when I started believing the truth that the Father wanted to speak to me through His Word, and the journey continues by drawing me closer to the Father. I am one of His sheep and He will speak to me and guide me. This journey will continue for the rest of my life here on the Earth, as I walk in being a daughter of the Father—or, as some would say, a daughter of the King.

CHAPTER TWO

God's
Love

How do you know God loves you?
Do you believe because you were told?
Do you question or wonder if you are loved?
Do you really believe God loves you?
Is God's love for you dependent on what
you've done or haven't done?
Is God's love something you long for?
Do you live feeling loved by God?

As the old song goes, "Jesus loves me, this I know, for the bible tells me so… Yes, Jesus loves me. Yes, Jesus loves me. Yes, Jesus loves me. The Bible tells me so." But I had so many questions about His love. I was one of those children who questioned and wondered if she was loved. I was one of those children who questioned everything. It didn't matter to me that the song said Jesus loved me because the Bible told me so; I wasn't sure that Jesus loved me.

I know my parents loved me, so the reasons why I questioned whether Jesus loved me are somewhat complicated. I was like a seesaw; one day I was up, and I was loved by God, and the next day I might be down, questioning God's love for me.

My questions about God's love had nothing to do with Him. It was all about how I felt. Whether I felt worthy to receive His love or not, that was the seesaw part. If I did good and felt that no one was upset with me, I decided that I must be okay in God's eyes. But if I felt that someone was upset with me, or that I didn't meet God's standard, I wasn't sure that He loved me. The lie was that the Father's love for me was conditional on my performance.

Who was I to tell God whether He loved me or not? It would be like having a child you love with all your heart coming to you and saying "Why don't you love me?" or "Do you love me now because I cleaned my room?"

My goodness, how I loved my children! It had nothing to do with how they performed on any given day. I loved my children unconditionally. Sometimes they frustrated me, or I feared for their well-being, but I never doubted my love for them. My hope was that they would know and believe that I loved them.

If I could love my children unconditionally, it seems so odd to me that I struggled with believing the Father could love me. I believed that God's love for me was proportionate to the amount of good I did. Now I know that it's foolish to believe that my good works could make me more loved by God. At the time, it was common for me to question God's love.

When I began to search out the Lord, wanting Him to be Lord of my life, my journey began. As I started reading the Bible, I read that God is love and that He loves us. I went to meetings where we sang about God's love, where people said "God loves you," and where I heard teachings on God's love. I even started saying the right words: "God loves me." And I would tell other people, "God loves you."

There was a big *but*. I still had those old questions in my mind—but, why, how come… I so wanted to believe that God loved me. Thoughts that I wasn't loved came often and I started to meditate on them. Maybe God didn't love me. Guilt, shame, and condemnation snuck in and spoke very loudly in my head.

One day as I was being ministered to by friends, I wondered about how God could love me if I had messed up and sinned. I asked for forgiveness and felt His loving peace wash over me. I felt so loved that day. Whatever needed doing in my heart, happened. My heart was healed that day and I believed God loved me. It was a revelation in the Spirit. God loved me! On my own, I couldn't believe it in my soul and spirit, but the Holy Spirit gave me a revelation of the Word that day so that I could believe. It became settled in my heart.

The truth became very clear that God loved me. It didn't matter what I did, and I didn't have to earn His love. He loved me. It was such a freedom! I no longer had to question God's love because of what I did. If I felt I did something wrong, the Father still loved me. If I did a good thing, the Father loved me.

He loves me in my imperfections. He loves me when I laugh. He loves me when I cry. He loves me when I fall. He loves me when I sin—and He always has. The enemy would like to make me feel guilty and tempt me to fall into the same trap of questioning God's love. I have no doubt anymore. I choose to stay close to the Lord and know that He loves me.

How do you know when the work is done? How do you when you believe not only in your head that God loves you but also in your spirit? When that happens, you don't question His love anymore. Your inner dialogue changes. It doesn't sound like "God must hate me. Look what I did. Oh, I'm sure He cannot possibly love me after today. How can He love me? Oh, I'm sure God loves me today… Yes, I think He loves me…" You need a judgment system to decide whether God loves you.

Jesus told the parable of the prodigal son. I think this parable was a way of showing us how loving our Father God is. In the story, a son wants his inheritance early. His father has no reason to give his son the inheritance, but he does. The son gladly takes it and leaves his father's house to make it in the world—but he squanders his inheritance away and ends up eating with the pigs. He then returns and tells the father that he has sinned and isn't worthy even to be called a son. But it turns out that his father has been patiently waiting for his son to return. He runs to meet him, embracing him with love. The father rejoiced that his son had returned. When the son said he was no longer worthy to be called a son, the father just put the best robe on him, placed a ring on his finger, and ordered the calf to be killed so they could eat and be merry.[3]

God the Father gives us everything. Just like the prodigal, though, we can choose to do our own thing, and sometimes that's not at all what the Father intends for us. He is patient and waits for us to return. When we return, He loves us and celebrates us.

The father in the parable never told his son that he wasn't good enough to return. He just embraced his son with all his love. Why? Because God's love covers over all our sins. The son then had a choice to receive the love offered to him. Whether or not he received it, the love was there for him—just like the love of God. Whether or not we choose to receive His love, *He loves us.* His love is there for us to receive whether we've earned it or not. His love for us has nothing to do with what we do.

---

3   The whole story can be found in Luke 15:11–24.

The love of God is a hard concept to grasp. Imagine that the God of the universe loves you. Why would He love you? The only way I could believe it for myself was by revelation knowledge. The Holy Spirit taught me through a revelation in my spirit that God loved me—and it wasn't just *knowledge*, it was a deep truth embedded in my spirit that no one could change. I remember the feeling of being completely surrounded by love, enveloped in the love of Christ. That feeling of love that no one can explain? I just know that it's the love of the Father.

John 3:16 is quoted so often: *"For God so loved the world that He gave His only begotten Son…"* (NKJV) I am part of that world. You are part of that world. My friends and family are part of that world. And God loves us all.

> *…that Christ may dwell in your hearts through faith; that you, being rooted and grounded in love, may be able to comprehend with all the saints what is the width and length and depth and height—to know the love of Christ which passes knowledge; that you may be filled with all the fullness of God.*
>
> —Ephesians 3:17–19, NKJV

Jesus wants us to know how wide, long, deep, and high His love is. I want to be filled with the fullness of God. The first step is inviting Christ to dwell in our hearts, which helps us to comprehend His love. The second step is to know the love of Christ which passes all knowledge. How does the love of Christ pass all knowledge? This happens when we quit intellectualizing His love and ask the Holy Spirit to give us revelation knowledge to know His love. The truth of His love then changes from a head knowledge to existing in our hearts, so that our whole beings can know His love.

Scripture tells us that God is love:

...for God is love. In this the love of God was made manifest (displayed) where we are concerned: in that God sent His Son, the only begotten or unique [Son], into the world so that we might live through Him. In this is love: not that we loved God, but that He loved us and sent His Son to be the propitiation (the atoning sacrifice) for our sins.

—1 John 4:8–10, AMPC

What kind of love is that? It's a love I could only understand by divine revelation.[4] God loved us and sent His Son to die for our sins, to set us free. Jesus was willing to give His life for us, and this action restored our ability to commune and have relationship with the Father. The Father knew we would need help, so He then sent the Holy Spirit to live on the Earth to be our helper, comforter, and advocate. He gives us gifts of the Holy Spirit and allows the fruit of the Holy Spirit to be manifested through us. God did all of that for me, and for you. That is love!

God is love and He tells us in scripture what love is. God is every aspect of what love is.

Love suffers long and is kind; love does not envy; love does not parade itself, is not puffed up; does not behave rudely, does not seek its own, is not provoked, thinks no evil; does not rejoice in iniquity, but rejoices in the truth; bears all things, believes all things, hopes all things, endures all things. Love never fails.

—1 Corinthians 13:4–8, NKJV

---

4   Understanding what was done at the cross would be a whole other book in itself.

Love is kind and does not think evil. If you hear unkind, evil thoughts about ourselves, seek the Lord and find out where those thoughts are coming from and what to do about them. Anything that doesn't witness to the loving character of God needs to be examined closely. The Holy Spirit corrects us, but those corrections are given in a loving and convicting way, not a harsh and condemning way.

Love suffers long. God is so loving and patient. We and others aren't so patient with ourselves, however.

> *Above all things have intense and unfailing love for one another, for love covers a multitude of sins [forgives and disregards the offenses of others].*
>
> —1 Peter 4:8, AMPC

God doesn't ask us to do things He doesn't do. He asks us to have intense, unfailing love for each other. Therefore, we can conclude that He has intense, unfailing love for us and His love covers a multitude of our sins.

> *No one has greater love [no one has shown stronger affection] than to lay down (give up) his own life for his friends.*
>
> —John 15:13, AMPC

> *But God shows and clearly proves His [own] love for us by the fact that while we were still sinners, Christ (the Messiah, the Anointed One) died for us.*
>
> —Romans 5:8, AMPC

> *But You, O Lord, are a God merciful and gracious, slow to anger and abounding in mercy and loving-kindness and truth.*
>
> —Psalm 86:15, AMPC

O give thanks to the Lord, for He is good; for His mercy and loving-kindness endure forever!

—1 Chronicles 16:34, AMPC

Oh, that men would praise [and confess to] the Lord for His goodness and loving-kindness and His wonderful works to the children of men! For He satisfies the longing soul and fills the hungry soul with good.

—Psalm 107:8–9, AMPC

Your mercy and loving-kindness, O Lord, extend to the skies, and Your faithfulness to the clouds.

—Psalm 36:5, AMPC

I have been crucified with Christ [in Him I have shared His crucifixion]; it is no longer I who live, but Christ (the Messiah) lives in me; and the life I now live in the body I live by faith in (by adherence to and reliance on and complete trust in) the Son of God, Who loved me and gave Himself up for me.

—Galatians 2:20, AMPC

See what [an incredible] quality of love the Father has given (shown, bestowed on) us, that we should [be permitted to] be named and called and counted the children of God! And so we are!

—1 John 3:1, AMPC

The earth, O Lord, is full of Your mercy and loving-kindness; teach me Your statutes.

—Psalm 119:64, AMPC

God's love is always there for us. It's up to me to embrace His love.

Joy fills my heart because I can say, "He loves me! He loves me just the way I am! He loves me!" And I can mean it.

The Lie:
I have to earn God's love.

The Truth:
God loves me. I don't have to do anything.
He just loves me.

My journey continues as I walk in the love of the Father, experiencing His love in greater depths and knowing and drawing closer to Him. When thoughts of an unloving nature come to my mind, I ask myself whether this is what a loving and heavenly Father would think towards me—or is it a lie from the enemy?

CHAPTER THREE

God's
Forgiveness

Does God forgive? How do you know?
What do I have to do to be forgiven?
Does God ever forget what we have done?
How can I just be forgiven?

The Bible is very clear that God forgives us. Christ sacrificed His life on the cross for the forgiveness of our sins.

And you, being dead in your trespasses and the uncircumcision of your flesh, He has made alive together with Him, having forgiven you all trespasses, having wiped out the handwriting of requirements that was against us, which was contrary to us. And He has taken it out of the way, having nailed it to the cross.

—Colossians 2:13–14, NKJV

You would probably agree with me that God forgives our sins. Yet throughout my life I have struggled with forgiveness, and I've witnessed many people struggle with feeling forgiven.

Now, stop and think of the worst thing you've ever done. Do you feel forgiven?

I didn't. The lies going through my head told me, "If anyone finds out what you did, they'll think you're awful. How can God love you? And if He doesn't love you, how can He forgive you?" In response, my head would say, "God forgives me." But my heart would say, "You're no good."

No matter what I had done, whether it was big or small, I kept it inside and believed that it made me an awful person, because I had done something against God. I knew in my head that God forgives, but my inner dialogue would go something like this: "Lord, please forgive me. How could I have done something so stupid? Why did I do that?" Then, weeks or months later, or years later, I'd think again, "Lord, please forgive me. I'm so sorry I did that. I'm so sorry I said that. What was I thinking? I know I never should have done that. Forgive me, Lord." Ten years later, I'd still be saying, "Forgive me, Lord. Could you please forgive me?"

The cycle continued. I asked forgiveness and then beat myself up at the same time. I thought I believed in forgiveness, but I would keep having the same inner dialogue with myself. Sometimes I wondered if I even wanted to be forgiven. I don't think I was able to believe that I could just be forgiven. The lying, tormenting voice of satan, the accuser of the brethren, kept coming back at me: "Has God really forgiven you? Look at you—you did it again! God remembers your sins. Do you think He forgets?"

This has to come from satan, because I don't believe the Lord would have told me I wasn't forgiven. It had to be satan—the liar, the thief, and the destroyer—or it could just have been my own self.

I couldn't fully understand that God forgives us, that when He does forgive our sin it is gone forever, washed away. The concept was foreign to me.

I remember once being told that God keeps a record of all the good things we do and all the bad things we do, and when we die hopefully the good is more numerous than the bad. I don't remember where I was taught this idea, but it sure stuck with me. This formed a truth in my heart, but it was a total lie. So I believed that God forgave my sins, but there was still a bad mark on my record. The truth is when God forgives us, all record of the sin is removed!

People hear things like this and then pass it on to others without knowing the truth of the Word of God. This is why we need our minds to be renewed and transformed by the Word. We are forgiven, loved, and washed clean from sin, but I couldn't understand how God could just forgive me and remove sin from my soul—my mind, will, and emotions.

What does the Word say?

> But if we walk in the light as He is in the light, we have fellowship with one another, and the blood of Jesus Christ His Son cleanses us from all sin… If we confess our sins, He is faithful and just to forgive us our sins and to cleanse us from all unrighteousness.
> —1 John 1:7, 9, NKJV (emphasis added)

> And from Jesus Christ the faithful and trustworthy Witness, the Firstborn of the dead [first to be brought back to life] and the Prince (Ruler) of the kings of the earth. To Him Who ever loves us and has once [for all] loosed and freed us from our sins by His own blood…
> —Revelation 1:5, AMPC

For You, O Lord, are good, and ready to forgive [our tres-
passes, sending them away, letting them go completely and
forever]; and You are abundant in mercy and loving-kind-
ness to all those who call upon You.

—Psalm 86:5, AMPC

[The Father] has delivered and drawn us to Himself out
of the control and the dominion of darkness and has trans-
ferred us into the kingdom of the Son of His love, in Whom
we have our redemption through His blood, [which means]
the forgiveness of our sins.

—Colossians 1:13–14, AMPC

After learning the Word and believing in forgiveness, I still sometimes experienced tormenting thoughts. Most of the time I felt forgiven, but sometimes I still fell into the temptation of questioning forgiveness.

One day, I heard a preacher speak about about James 5:16. He explained that if you confess your sin to someone, satan doesn't have any right to hold it against you; you are forgiven. And you can use this scripture to fight back at satan:

Therefore, confess your sins to one another, and pray for one
another so that you may be healed. The effective prayer of a
righteous man can accomplish much.

—James 5:16, NASB

I decided that I would find someone and confess my sin to them, even though I had begged God many times to forgive me. I confessed, they prayed, and I chose to believe that I was forgiven. There have been times when I've asked for forgiveness and felt God's love washing over me, flooding my soul. I had no doubt that God's total forgiveness of my sins was real.[5]

Afterward, when the enemy came and told me, "Look, you did that. That was a sin," I would say, "I confessed and I am forgiven." I used the Word to fight the lie. I made the decision to believe the truth that God forgives.

You may ask, does it work? Yes, it works, I chose to believe what the Word of God says rather than what I or the devil says about the matter. I repented with all my heart and was forgiven.

When my old inner dialogue comes back, I turn from the lie that I'm not forgiven and simply speak the truth that I *am* forgiven, that the Lord has forgiven me, and that through the blood of Jesus my sins are washed away. My heart was healed, and I was touched by the love of God. I chose to believe what the word says: I am forgiven.

Do I feel forgiven?

Do I feel different?

Have the lies stopped?

I felt so loved and forgiven that day. I never doubted whether I had been forgiven for that situation again. I felt the loving arms and embrace of God. All the guilt, shame, and condemnation left me.

I was once asked if I believe the sacrifice of Jesus was enough for me. Who was I not to accept Christ's death on the cross for my sins and say that it wasn't good enough? Another truth came to me that day. Being forgiven has nothing to do with what I do; it's all about *Him*. Christ did it at the cross. He died so that I may be forgiven. It's my choice to believe and

---

5   I don't look for this feeling every time I repent, but God knew I needed it then. Just remember that you *are* forgiven, whether you feel it or not.

accept that Christ died on the cross for me, for my sins and the sins of the world.

Therefore, do I always feel forgiven?

Yes and no. Sometimes when God forgives me, and I confess, a feeling of great love and peace surrounds me and the presence of the Holy Spirit washes over me. Other times I just know and believe by faith in the Word of God that I am forgiven. But I always feel peace and truth in my mind. Forgiveness by Christ isn't a feeling; it's a sacrifice, an act of love. The love of God.

> *For God did not send the Son into the world in order to judge (to reject, to condemn, to pass sentence on) the world, but that the world might find salvation and be made safe and sound through Him.*
>
> —John 3:17, AMPC

Many books have been written about God's forgiveness and the cross, but I am thankful to our Lord that He made it so simple for us. He continually reassures me of His love and forgiveness in His Word.

Do I always go to others and confess when I sin? No. I often say "Oh Lord, forgive me" and just believe. For most little things I just say, "Sorry, Lord" and move on. Other times I still struggle with feeling free. I go to a friend, do as the Word says, and confess my faults one to another.

Often when I'm struggling with forgiveness, it's because I have some unforgiveness in me and need healing within my heart. When I ask the Father where I'm hurting and why, He reveals to me a deep wound in my heart. He will heal my woundedness in layers, showing me one thing and then later showing me another pertaining to the same event. I need to forgive others their part... and forgive myself my part. When

I do that, I know I'm free. I just tell the enemy, "I confessed, get out," and I refuse to believe that I'm not forgiven.

Will God forgive us more than once?

One day as I was asking the Lord to forgive me, my inner dialogue went something like this: "Lord, I'm so sorry. I did it again. Can you forgive me again? How many times will I do this? Will you please forgive me." I then got the feeling that the Holy Spirit was speaking to me, saying, "If I ask you to forgive seventy times seven, why do you think I wouldn't do that and more for you?"

> *Then Peter came up to Him and said, Lord, how many times may my brother sin against me and I forgive him and let it go? [As many as] up to seven times?*
> *Jesus answered him, I tell you, not up to seven times, but seventy times seven!*
> —Matthew 18:21–22, AMPC

Wow! What an awesome forgiving God we serve. As soon as we humble ourselves and ask forgiveness, He offers us His forgiveness and our sin is wiped away—many, many times, over and over. The Father never asks us to do something He wouldn't do.

So why wait to ask for forgiveness?

Sometimes I get frustrated because I'll do or say something that maybe did not come from a right heart attitude. Or I might say something that isn't uplifting. Then I beat myself up for a while and hear the same inner dialogue: "Why did I do that? I know better. That was so stupid of me. People will think I'm a bad Christian. Lord, I want to be a good example. I want to shine with you and do the things you do."

Now, does it help to beat yourself up for hours or days or weeks and then repent and accept forgiveness? Why not just confess it right away and go on walking in the truth and light of Christ? There is no condemnation for those who are in Christ. Therefore, after I've asked forgiveness I also ask the Holy Spirit to heal any hurt in my heart and any hurt and pain that the other person is feeling. I may also ask for a revelation about why I feel the way I'm feeling and why I choose to react a certain way: "Father, help me to understand what's in my heart causing me to act and say the things I do."

We all sin and fall short of the glory of God. I'm so grateful that we have such a loving Father who forgives. Because we have such a loving God, who forgives and forgives, we must be careful that we don't use this an excuse to keep sinning. The more love for God we have in our hearts, the more we know that we are loved by Him, and the less we will want to sin. Out of our love for the Lord, we will want to do the right thing.

I cannot emphasize enough that as we are healed, delivered, and set free, our lives change from glory to glory. The sooner we go to Jesus for forgiveness, the sooner satan loses his foothold on us. Just pray, "Lord, you did it at the cross for me. I'm not holding on to this. I'm giving to you everything I've done. Forgive me. Thanks for your forgiveness."

> *The Lord your God is in the midst of you, a Mighty One, a Savior [Who saves]! He will rejoice over you with joy; He will rest [in silent satisfaction] and in His love He will be silent and make no mention [of past sins, or even recall them]; He will exult over you with singing.*
> —Zephaniah 3:17, AMPC

God forgives our sins and doesn't remember them. They're gone.

The Lie:
You're not really forgiven because God
keeps track of your sins.

The Truth:
Christ died on the cross for all my sin. I am forgiven
and my sins are gone, forgotten.

The journey continues as I go on walking in Christ, knowing that He sacrificed Himself for all my sins, and all my sins still to come, so that I may approach the Father and receive forgiveness. I must continue to walk in forgiveness, without guilt and condemnation.

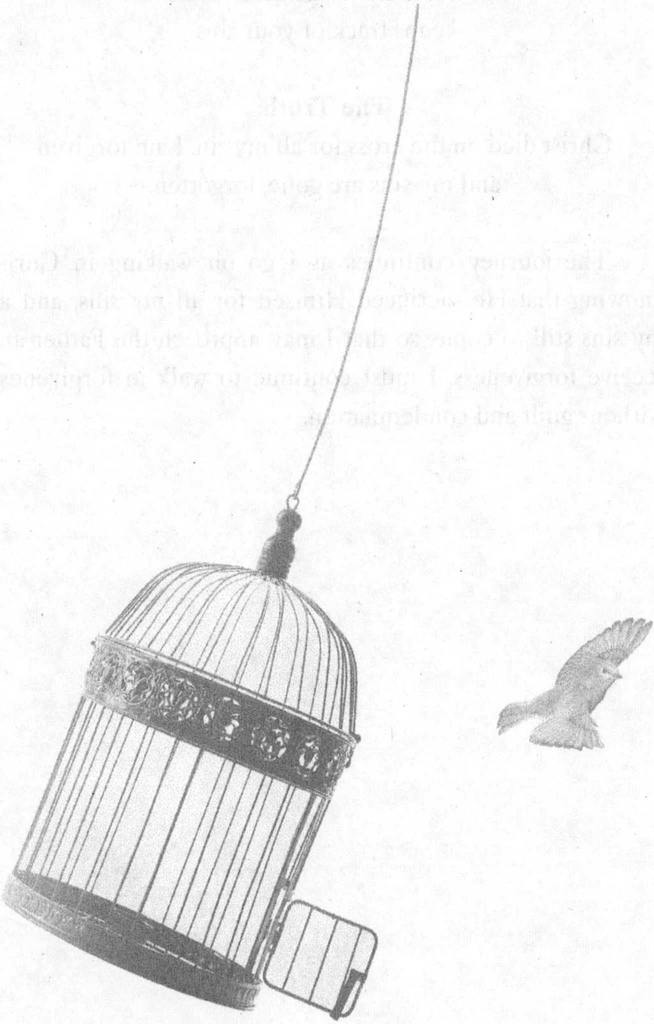

CHAPTER FOUR

Forgiving Yourself

Do you forgive yourself when others won't forgive you?
Have you ever done something to someone
who then held it over your head?
Has a loved one ever held a sin over you?
Do you feel it's your job to help that person forgive you?
Are you trapped in self-condemnation if
someone won't forgive you?
Do you fear the backlash of their unforgiveness?
Do you try to change for that person, hoping
they will forgive you?

I've watched so many people suffer because someone wouldn't forgive them. I've known husbands who were never able to forgive themselves for a mistake because their wives wouldn't forgive them. I've seen wives cry with anguish at not being able to be forgiven by their husbands. I've known children who had no families because they made a mistake and weren't allowed to come home. I've wept with devastated parents whose children refused to forgive them. Friendships break because of misunderstandings, and because of unforgiveness.

I would say that I forgive myself, but I try hard to feel forgiven by others. In reality, deep down I have struggled with forgiving myself.

As I listen to what goes through my thoughts, I receive a revelation of the truth I'm living. Somehow I formed a stronghold in my mind dictating that if someone doesn't forgive me, it's my fault. I must therefore do something to help others forgive me. Or I've lived with the idea that I can't be forgiven by God because others won't forgive me.

It's very interesting to figure out how we formed these ideas in our heads. Because I believed something that was so false, I spent my life walking in fear that I might offend someone by saying or doing something they wouldn't forgive me for. I was fearful of others, giving the enemy a foothold into my life. I perceived that I was not forgiven, which led to inner dialogue that went something like this: "Lord, why cannot they forgive me? Help me, Lord. What do I do? How can I get them to forgive me? I never meant to hurt them. Lord, why can't they see the real me? What can I do to be forgiven? Lord, forgive me." The inner dialogue becomes sinful in nature when it starts to judge or ridicule others: "They do lots of wrong things, too, and I forgive them. Can't they see themselves and what they do, Lord?"

When thinking about forgiveness, it is necessary to go to the Word. What does the Word say? The Word says that He forgives and that our forgiveness isn't related to what others think. It's very important to remember that you aren't responsible for getting others to forgive you. That isn't your job. That's between them and God. You are only responsible for your own actions and reactions. Your responsibility ends when you ask for your own wrongs to be forgiven.

The scripture does say we should go to our brother and ask forgiveness. The Lord may ask you to try and ask the other person's forgiveness for your wrongdoing, or perceived wrongdoing. It's wonderful when forgiveness is given, but it can be very hurtful when it isn't. This can disrupt and destroy families, friendships, marriages, and churches. It can also destroy the person who is asking for forgiveness.

I have learned that we never know what others are thinking in their heart. We may think they haven't truly forgiven, but who are we to judge? Do I know what is happening in another person's heart? Only God knows.

Other times, people may not extend forgiveness to you. We don't know why. There could be many reasons. They could be trying to forgive with all their heart, yet inside they are hurting and angry and wounded. It may take a while for them to forgive and let go.

The main issue here is to remember that your forgiveness only comes from the Lord. Yes, we forgive one another, but our sinful words and deeds are forgiven by the Lord by His atoning sacrifice on the cross.

As we accept God's forgiveness for our sins and quit focussing on others, we can begin to pray for them with love. When people cannot forgive, it's often because they need to be healed in their hearts. Perhaps you touched a sore spot or did something to hurt them. When we believe that God has forgiven us, we have empathy for others. We can pray for healing of their hearts, pray for God's love to touch them, pray that God will show them the condition of their hearts, pray that they will be able to forgive, and most of all pray for God to bless them.

Scripture tells us to pray for our enemies. You might not see others as enemies, but if they aren't for you, they are against you.

> *But I tell you, Love your enemies and pray for those who persecute you…*
>
> —Matthew 5:44, AMPC

Is there someone in your life who you believe has not forgiven you? Does beating yourself up help them to forgive? Does all the worrying and revisiting the situation help them to forgive?

Satan would love for us not to forgive one another. He wants to hold people's sins over them. Whether it's control, unforgiveness, hurt, rejection, stubbornness, or ill will on their part, know in the depth of your spirit that you are forgiven. It's God's job to deal with the other person, not you. Place them in the Lord's hand. Get yourself right with God. You might have sinned and fallen short, but Christ forgives all sins.

It becomes very hard to forgive yourself and receive God's forgiveness when others hold your sins over you and won't forgive you. I hated that. But it helped me to realize how important it is to forgive others and never hold their sins over them. I believe that's why we are asked to forgive one another, to set them free to receive God's forgiveness—and to set us free from offense, bitterness, and anger.

When other people didn't forgive me, I let their unforgiveness bother me, both in my mind and heart. Dwelling on them consumed too much of my time. I so wanted to feel loved by them. I wanted to have good relationships with people. I was very good at blaming myself for everything and believing that if I was somehow different, they would forgive me or I wouldn't be in the mess I thought I was in. This kept my mind and thoughts away from what the Lord was trying to tell me. It caused me to think ill of myself, something the Lord would never want me to do.

> *And become useful and helpful and kind to one another, tenderhearted (compassionate, understanding, loving-hearted), forgiving one another [readily and freely], as God in Christ forgave you.*
>
> —Ephesians 4:32, AMPC

> *If we confess our sins, He is faithful and just to forgive us our sins and to cleanse us from all unrighteousness.*
>
> —1 John 1:9, NKJV

> *I, even I, am He who blots out your transgressions for My own sake; and I will not remember your sins.*
>
> —Isaiah 43:25, NKJV

> *Bless the Lord, O my soul; and all that is within me, bless His holy name! Bless the Lord, O my soul, and forget not all His benefits: who forgives all your iniquities, who heals all your diseases…*
>
> —Psalm 103:1–3, NKJV

> *The thief does not come except to steal, and to kill, and to destroy. I have come that they may have life, and that they may have it more abundantly.*
>
> —John 10:10, NKJV

The Lie:

If people won't forgive you, God won't forgive you.

The Truth:

God forgives and we must forgive ourselves
whether others forgive us or not.

The journey continues as I walk in the forgiveness and love of the Father, not looking to others but to Him. Most importantly, I must remember to forgive myself, allowing the Father to love me, forgive me, help me, guide me, counsel me, and be my Father.

CHAPTER FIVE

Forgiving Others

Why should we forgive others?
Why should we forgive them for what they've done?
Do we think they deserve our forgiveness?
How many times have they hurt us?

Forgiving others has never been a problem for me. I've always known from the depth of my core that I needed to forgive. I was taught by my parents that there is no question: you must forgive others. Therefore, forgiveness has been part of life. It's something you just do.

The problem, I realized, is that it was easy for me to say "I forgive..." That was just a matter of fact. You never questioned it. You just forgave. I saw and heard people forgive others for the not so nice things that happened to them. Having these examples made it easy for me to know the importance of forgiving people.

As I read the Word and spent time in prayer, Bible study, and church meetings, I noticed something in the core of my being, my heart. Even though I had forgiven a person, when I thought about the situation or talked about it, the peace in my heart was disturbed.

Yes, I had learned about forgiveness, but I believed that when I forgave someone for something they'd done to me, it would all be gone. Often it was gone, never to be thought of again. Then there were times when, no matter how much I said "Lord, I forgive them," my inner dialogue of self-condemnation started up. I'd ask myself, "How could they treat me that way? Why did they do that? Didn't they know how much that would hurt me? Why don't they look at themselves?" Or I would go into pity party mode, thinking, "You don't treat people you love like that. They must not love me. If I had done everything right, they wouldn't hurt me. What's wrong with me?"

Oh, but I forgave them—as best I could. I just needed a healed heart so that I could forgive with my heart instead of my head.

Why should you forgive with your heart? Because the core of your being is in your heart, and the scripture tells us to do so.

So also My heavenly Father will deal with every one of you if you do not freely forgive your brother from your heart his offenses.
—Matthew 18:35, AMPC (emphasis added)

You need to forgive with your heart because that's where the hurt is. When someone hurts you, your heart hurts.

When I couldn't forgive someone, or when I thought I had forgiven them but my thought life proved otherwise, I knew that I needed healing—healing in my heart.

He heals the brokenhearted and binds up their wounds [curing their pains and their sorrows].
—Psalm 147:3, AMPC

The Lord is close to those who are of a broken heart and saves such as are crushed with sorrow for sin and are humbly and thoroughly penitent.

—Psalm 34:18, AMPC

It was a new thing for me to be healed in my heart. I'd just thought you said "I forgive you" and the offence was gone. That's forgiveness from the mind, not the heart. Scripture says that God heals the brokenhearted (Isaiah 61:1)

First, you must admit that you have a broken heart. It's very easy to say, "I'm okay. I'm fine. That didn't bother me... I just forgive." Again, listen to your inner dialogue and watch out for what your heart is feeling when a person you need to forgive comes to mind. Sometimes it may be a group of people, a government, or a generational iniquity that's been passed down. When my thoughts turned to anything but pure and loving thoughts, I knew I hadn't fully forgiven someone. I still had to look at my heart.

Forgiveness was a process for me. I would ask God to pray for my broken heart, to search my heart. I was so thankful that I had wonderful people to help me pray for my broken heart, and to be honest with me and guide me in seeing the unforgiveness.

...pray one for another, that you may be healed.

—James 5:16, NKJV

Therefore encourage (admonish, exhort) one another and edify (strengthen and build up) one another, just as you are doing.

—1 Thessalonians 5:11, AMPC

Step by step, issue by issue, I noticed that I truly began to forgive. I could talk about what had happened and not feel grieved in my heart. Instead I would feel compassion and peace for the other person. I knew that if I tried in my head to believe I had forgiven them, I would still feel grieved in my heart. I would need further heart healing in order to forgive.

I believe that God honours our willingness to forgive, and as we grow He helps us to get healed so we can truly forgive and let things go so the Lord can deal with them.

Therefore, how do I know if I haven't forgiven a person? If I think of what someone did to me, or didn't do, and it stirs up any kind of emotional hurt or negative thinking, I would say there is probably some unforgiveness there.

When God washes us, our sins are gone. When we ask for forgiveness, God forgives us and it is forgotten. If we keep bringing up something that another person did to us, and if we keep talking about it over and over, there is still unforgiveness left to deal with.[6] Once we forgive someone, we shouldn't still be holding that sin over them.

Another clue that you probably haven't forgiven a person is when your thoughts and words about them aren't said in love. If you've truly forgiven, you don't wait for opportunities to report about what they've done. And when you're sitting idle, do you think vengeful thoughts about someone? If so, you haven't forgiven them.

These are ways in which you can check your heart. If any of these points are true in your heart or mind, you can be pretty sure that you've tried to forgive with your head—not your heart.

So how can you forgive with more than just your head? Personally, I could only forgive from the core of my heart once the hurt of the pain inflicted on me was healed. When the

---

6   It's different when you share God's healing and He mentions incidents from your life.

Holy Spirit touched my heart and healed my woundedness, I was able to forgive from my heart.

Knowing the truth in the Word of God makes it easier to forgive. Sometimes I found it hard to forgive because I had lost something and couldn't get it back—or at least that's what I thought. Then I was reminded in the Word that God is my provider and vindicator.

> *And my God will liberally supply (fill to the full) your every need according to His riches in glory in Christ Jesus.*
> —Philippians 4:19, AMPC

> *But no weapon that is formed against you shall prosper, and every tongue that shall rise against you in judgment you shall show to be in the wrong. This [peace, righteousness, security, triumph over opposition] is the heritage of the servants of the Lord [those in whom the ideal Servant of the Lord is reproduced]; this is the righteousness or the vindication which they obtain from Me [this is that which I impart to them as their justification], says the Lord.*
> —Isaiah 54:17, AMPC

In the end, forgiveness is a choice. You must choose to forgive, and when you choose and still struggle, you need to seek the Lord for healing.

God is so good. He waits until we're ready and then reveals our hearts to us, teaches us new lessons, and heals our hearts at a deep level.

Here's an example. I loved my mother totally, and as an adult I forgave her for things she had knowingly and unknowingly did that caused hurt in my heart. I believed that I had nothing against my mom in any way, and when I spoke of her it was with honour and respect. As an adult, I understood what she had gone through in life and used it to rationalize why I should forgive her.

One day while in prayer ministry, the subject of my mom came up and I was asked what I had missed as a young girl. My heart broke open and I started crying. The things I had wanted and needed from her but hadn't gotten came pouring out. I was then taken to a new level of forgiveness, to forgive her from the perspective of a child, not the adult I had become. Jesus then came to heal the brokenhearted child within me. Because I had honoured and respected my mom so much, because I had truly loved her and wanted her love in return, I had been unable to look at that hurt in my heart. If you'd asked me if I had unforgiveness in my heart towards my mother, I would have said, "Definitely not. I have forgiven her." But when the Lord revealed the broken, wounded heart I'd suffered as a child, I could forgive with greater measure. I was able to give the Lord all the things I had lost. I understood how I had been affected emotionally by my mom's busyness. Giving my hurt to the Lord and offering forgiveness allowed my heart to be healed, and it allowed the Father to pour His love into the place of my heart that had been broken, restoring it with His love. My heart went from woundedness to the Father's love.

As I reflected on my mother during this prayer time, I realized that I wouldn't have known the depth of hurt inside me without the Holy Spirit's revelation. I am continually amazed that I don't need to go digging for things in my heart; I can wait for the Lord to draw it to my attention. The Lord gives me revelations of different areas of my heart and how I need to let Him in to heal it so I can walk in a new measure of forgiveness.

Is it painful to deal with hurt and unforgiveness? What are the results of dealing with our heart? Yes, forgiveness and healing can be painful, but the Holy Spirit is so loving and gentle and the final result is greater peace, love, and joy. I can then become the person God created me to be and have greater love for my Saviour, Jesus. And I can also have greater love for the person who hurt me.

The other issue I needed to get over in order for me to walk in total forgiveness and freedom was condemnation. Satan would fill my mind with thoughts like "Oh, you're a Christian… and you still have *that* in your heart? How embarrassing. What kind of Christian are you? What are people going to think of you, knowing you have unforgiveness inside? You can't have any unforgiveness if you're a Christian."

With all my heart, I have tried to walk in forgiveness and I still have stuff that I need to deal with. My choice now is to either deal with the stuff or hide it.

The Lord asks us to forgive seventy times seven. I'm sure He knew we would be called to forgive many times and in many different ways. For me, I started with head forgiveness and then slowly got to the place where I could completely forgive from the heart.

What does scripture say about forgiveness?

One of the most important truths I know today is that the Lord will forgive me. The Lord's Prayer says, *"And forgive us our sins, for we also forgive everyone who is indebted to us"* (Luke 11:4, NKJV). This is the one condition that is placed on how we will be forgiven. The verse doesn't say that we won't be forgiven, but that we will be forgiven in the same way we forgive others. Oh my! I want to be totally forgiven, so I know what I must do. I must totally forgive others.

I'm sure that the Holy Spirit will reveal other areas in my life where I need to forgive at a deeper level. When that happens, I'm confident the Holy Spirit will be the healer of my heart as I choose to forgive from a deeper level or different perspective.

When God forgives us, the sin is gone. Forgotten. We are washed clean. When we forgive others, we should want the offense to be forgiven in the same—washed clean.

For if you forgive people their trespasses [their reckless and willful sins, leaving them, letting them go, and giving up resentment], your heavenly Father will also forgive you.
—Matthew 6:14, AMPC

Pay attention and always be on your guard [looking out for one another]. If your brother sins (misses the mark), solemnly tell him so and reprove him, and if he repents (feels sorry for having sinned), forgive him.
—Luke 17:3, AMPC

The Lie:
I just need to say "I forgive."

The Truth:
You need to forgive others from your heart.

The journey continues as I allow the Father to show me what's in my heart. I open my heart and emotions to be healed and then to forgive others from the depth of my heart. As long as I journey on the Earth, I will need to forgive.

CHAPTER SIX

Anger

Is anger wrong?
Should we get angry?
What do we do when we have that anger feeling?
Did God create us to feel this emotion?
Should we ignore our anger and hope it goes away?

Anger was a difficult emotion to acknowledge in my life. I believed I was never allowed to be angry. I just had to ignore it and believe I would be okay. All that hurt had to go somewhere, though, so I buried it deep within my heart.

I was blessed to have a friend tell me that I had anger in my heart, and that I spoke in an angry tone. I didn't think this was true. Perhaps I spoke firmly and in an opinionated way, but not angrily. This was a shock to me, because I knew that I worked hard at not being angry. Stated a different way, I had done my best to bury the emotion, thinking that I was pleasing God by not being angry.

In prayer, the Lord told me that I had suppressed my anger. He asked me to look up anger in the dictionary. This is what I found: "the feeling one has toward something that hurts, opposes, offends, annoys; wrath; strong displeasure."[7]

That wasn't the way I would define anger. Going by this definition, how could anyone not have anger in their life? Everyone experiences feelings of annoyance and displeasure. I certainly did, since I had lot of hurt feelings.

I had thought anger meant lashing out, yelling, throwing things, and saying harmful words meant to hurt others. What a deception! Anger is a feeling, not an action. There are ways that people express their anger, but what is the feeling behind the action? I had so often been told, "Don't be angry." What I was really being told was that I shouldn't have feelings.

I like how the Message Bible talks about anger:

Go ahead and be angry. You do well to be angry—but don't use your anger as fuel for revenge. And don't stay angry. Don't go to bed angry. Don't give the Devil that kind of foothold in your life.

—Ephesians 4:26–27, MSG

We need to acknowledge that we do get angry feelings and deal with the anger. Saying we aren't angry when we really are can give the devil a foothold. Why? Because we haven't dealt with the underlying emotion. It's still there, stuffed down deep. We often don't even realize it. So we're giving the enemy a foothold to lie, steal, and destroy, all the while thinking that we're doing the right thing by ignoring our anger.

Again, it's such a deceptive lie.

How does this work? I am not to ignore my anger, yet I am not to stay angry.

---

7 *Dictionary of Canadian English—The Senior Dictionary* (Toronto, ON: W.J. Gage Ltd., 1967), 42.

Imagine that you cut your hand with an unclean object and just ignore the cut. You tell yourself, "Oh, it's nothing." On the outside, the cut looks okay. You put a bandage on it. Then it starts getting red and full of pus. The hand swells, but you still think, "This is nothing. I'm fine. It'll go away." Eventually you need to go to the doctor because your hand has been infected and you need antibiotics.

Could anger be like this? When you're hurt, you put a bandage on it, thinking that you're okay. You try to cover up the hurt. Eventually other hurts enter the heart and fester, poisoning the heart, but you still think it's nothing. The cut on your hand gives you evidence that your body is being poisoned, but what evidence do your mind and emotions have that they are being poisoned by anger?

Listen to your thoughts. Anger that doesn't get dealt with produces unforgiveness, judgment, negative thoughts about yourself and others, and words which poison your mind and affect the way you talk, whether you know it or not. It can't be treated by antibiotics, but it can be treated with the healing love of the Father as the anger gets acknowledged and exposed.

Anger only leaves if you deal with it. We can mask it, but take the mask off and watch the anger explode. How do you deal with anger?

The first step is to acknowledge that you're angry: "Father, I'm angry and hurt. I'm giving you my anger and the situation that has made me angry. I'm casting my care onto you so you can take care of me." At first, though, I couldn't even use the word *angry*. Instead I used words like hurt, wounded, offended, and broken.

Just because you acknowledge your feelings of anger doesn't mean your situation will change—but you will. You will invite the Father to help you deal with your heart and the underlying situation.

I remember thinking, *How can I not go to bed angry? The situation that's making me angry isn't going to change.* So I would just grin and bear it, but in reality I was hurting and trying not to react inside. When I didn't know how to deal with the hurt, it became easy to take the feelings to another level, saying and thinking things I would later regret. Stuffing down anger often leads to an event that causes a person to explode.

Acknowledging your anger and giving it to the Lord, allowing Him to heal and transform anger into peace in your heart, shifts your thinking so that the eyes of your heart can see the situation with a peaceful attitude. The enemy no longer has a foothold to torment you. The situation in your life may not change, but your heart and level of peace will.

Ask God to give you a revelation of any anger you unknowingly, or knowingly, have in your heart. Ask Him how He wants you to deal with this anger.

This was unquestionably a process for me. I wanted to deal with anger because the Father tells us in His Word to get rid of it. But how? I prayed, expressing that I required His support to expose and heal the anger.

The process began. In dealing with the poison of anger in my heart, I had to start by forgiving, acknowledging that I had been hurt, giving that pain to the Lord, and allowing the Holy Spirit to heal my heart. The main indicator that I had the anger buried down deep was that I could feel it inside and tried to control it by faking happiness. The other indicator was the sharpness of my tone of voice. The biggest indicator I now have is recognizing hurt and knowing that it means anger is lurking inside, whether I believe it or not.

The process continues. We live in a world where we have to deal with people, ourselves, and our surroundings. And we will be angry. Stuffed-down anger festers in our hearts, affecting ourselves and those around us.

The lie I believed was that it was a sin to feel anger. I had told myself that I was never angry, but it was a huge lie. The truth I now know is that we undoubtedly feel anger, but what we do with it is of most importance. Why? Because what is in the heart comes out.

Paul told the Christians to get rid of anger. Why would he tell them to get rid of anger? He must have known that we would experience that emotion.

Getting rid of something isn't the same as ignoring it.

One day I thought of anger and compared it to storing items down in the basement. These are items I should deal with and get rid of, but instead I put them downstairs where I can ignore them. When I do this, the basement turns into a mess. Too many undealt-with emotions get to be a mess in your heart as well.

But now put away and rid yourselves [completely] of all these things: anger, rage, bad feeling toward others, curses and slander, and foulmouthed abuse and shameful utterances from your lips!

—Colossians 3:8, AMPC

"Be angry, and do not sin": do not let the sun go down on your wrath, nor give place to the devil... Let all bitterness, wrath, anger, clamor, and evil speaking be put away from you, with all malice. And be kind to one another, tender-hearted, forgiving one another, even as God in Christ forgave you.

—Ephesians 4:26–27, 31–32, NKJV

When I read the following scriptures, I'm reminded that the Lord also experiences the emotion of anger. If the Lord gets angry, but is slow to anger, then it must be an emotion we were created to experience as well.

> *The Lord is gracious and full of compassion, slow to anger and abounding in mercy and loving-kindness.*
>
> —Psalm 145:8, AMPC

> *The Lord is long-suffering and slow to anger, and abundant in mercy and loving-kindness...*
>
> —Numbers 14:18, AMPC

> *And when He had looked around at them with anger, being grieved by the hardness of their hearts...*
>
> —Mark 3:5, NKJV

> *But You are God, ready to pardon, gracious and merciful, slow to anger, abundant in kindness, and did not forsake them.*
>
> —Nehemiah 9:17, NKJV

> *He who is slow to anger is better than the mighty, and he who rules his spirit than he who takes a city.*
>
> —Proverbs 16:32, NKJV

> *So then, my beloved brethren, let every man be swift to hear, slow to speak, slow to wrath; for the wrath of man does not produce the righteousness of God.*
>
> —James 1:19–20, NKJV

The Lie:
I am not to be angry. I should just go on and forget
my angry emotions because they're wrong. I
should just say, "I'm okay."

The Truth:
Be angry, but do not sin. In other words, deal with
your anger. Acknowledge your feelings. The Father is
concerned about all your heart's feelings.

The journey continues as I acknowledge all my feelings
to the Father, who loves me and calls me His daughter. I will
continue to have angry, hurtful feelings, but my Father God
will heal my broken heart. Situations don't go away, but the
festering poison can be healed. As long as I continue on my
life journey, I will need to deal with anger.

CHAPTER SEVEN

God Listens and Cares About My Feelings

What if I were to confide how I feel?
Would I be judged and rejected?
Would I just be saying what I felt?
Would I just be expressing an opinion about
what was bugging me?

As a youngster, I concluded that I should just put my chin up, that I didn't have the right to have any hurt feelings. I was supposed to forgive, love my neighbour, trust God, and be joyful. It's interesting how easily this kind of attitude can be taught and learned. It seems to pass from one generation to the next. The message is that we should be strong within ourselves. Who wants to listen to your feelings? Who even cares about how you feel?

Unlearning this was a challenge for me!

I grew up feeling that I wasn't supposed to express my concerns or feelings—unless they were loving. As an adult, I now sit back and wonder, was I really told not to share my concerns and feelings or did I just perceive it? In the end, it doesn't matter how I developed the attitude of keeping my feelings to myself; it was there. I believed that I needed to just be a good Christian and not worry about how I felt. I believed that God would just look after me. I could only have one emotion: joyfulness. After all, I thought that was what the Lord expected of us.

While at a retreat, we were given the task of building a house that represented how the Father saw us. I built my house while asking God to show me what to do. Then I built a separate room in the house with no door. There was no way to access this room. In it I placed a sad face and a crying face. Focussed on the task at hand, the meaning of the room wasn't immediately important.

When the time came to share about our houses, I asked the Father what that room was all about. He responded by telling me it represented my belief that it was wrong to tell Him about my deep feelings of hurt and pain. Upon pondering this, I realized although God wanted me to experience joy, peace, love, and gladness, for most of my life I had thought having hurt feelings was wrong. If your heart is stuffed with feelings of hurt, and it's all trapped inside because you're afraid to express it, how can the Father fill you with all of His love?

What a revelation. I had talked to the Father on various occasions about some of my feelings when they came up, but I hadn't realized I had such a deep fear of admitting my sadness.

One helpful tool in releasing my feelings to the Father was getting a feelings chart. I didn't even have the vocabulary to express my feelings. As I would look at the feelings chart, I'd become able to tell the Father I was feeling lonely, abandoned, betrayed, frustrated, annoyed, insecure, unsure, anxious, relieved, excited, regretful, unworthy, embarrassed, fearful, ashamed, shocked, intimidated, etc. The list could go on. I still use the feeling chart to help me talk to God about my feelings. As I surrender my feelings to Him, He can heal my brokenness.

One day as I was ministering to a friend, I asked my friend to tell me about some of the good feelings he had about the situation we were talking about. He hesitated. After our time of ministry, he told me that classifying emotions as either good or bad always made him hesitate. He had learned that it was okay to have emotions, but classifying them as good or bad made him almost not want to share at all. After all, why would you want to share if your emotions are "bad"? Emotions are neither good or bad; they're just emotions, and acknowledging them is a first step toward being healed.

So I exchanged a lie for the truth. No emotions are wrong. It's how we deal with them that's important.

What does this have to do with God caring for us? Everything. Does God really care? I've often asked myself this question, and I used to answer, "Of course He cares." But I don't think my heart believed that. What I was really trying to ask was, "Does God care if I'm lonely, disappointed, frustrated, angry, or annoyed?"

When a friend of mine died, I sensed the Lord telling me not to ask why. So I never did. I just believed that this was life and I needed to ignore how I was feeling. God was in control, and who was I to question Him? Now, questioning God and asking Him to help with feelings and hurts in your heart are two different issues, but I saw them as the same.

Did I ignore my feelings because I felt I was supposed to? Yes, I really believed that I was just supposed to be strong in the Lord.

Did I ignore my feelings because I was so used to ignoring my feelings? Again, I had the Lord, and I believed He would be my strength. I believed all my grief could be stuffed down because God knew about my situation. My head was very good at rationalizing my beliefs. If I'm honest, though,

I ignored my feelings because I believed that my feelings weren't important and that God didn't really care about my feelings. I was supposed to be glad that my friend was with the Lord. I wasn't supposed to feel sadness, because the joy of the Lord was my strength.

Did I ignore my feelings because I simply didn't know how to deal with them? How can you deal with your feelings if you believe you're not supposed to feel anything but joy and thankfulness?

Or maybe, just maybe, I felt that I wasn't allowed to express my feelings. Maybe this held more truth than I chose to believe at the time. I was very good at expressing my opinions, but deep down I truly believed I wasn't allowed to express my feelings to the Lord—unless He brought up that I needed to deal with something. Then it was His decision to talk about and deal with my feelings. I could express my thoughts to God and question Him about many things, but I couldn't go to Him as a friend and tell Him the deep sadness I was feeling, at least not without Holy Spirit prompting me.

One weekend when we were attending a conference, I told God, "You know, my friend would have really enjoyed this conference and being here with us." I heard this reply: "You don't think she is enjoying where she is." My inner dialogue went something like this: "I guess I'm just being selfish, thinking of me. I shouldn't be thinking this way." What I probably meant, and didn't know how to express, is this: "Lord, I really miss my friend. I loved travelling and sharing with her. I miss our talks, our praying together, and I feel a huge sense of loneliness, isolation, and abandonment."

Eventually the Lord and I did have this conversation and I was able to grieve and be healed of the sadness in my heart. I remember that day very clearly. It happened about three years later. I just started crying and asked, "Lord, why am I crying?" He said, "You are missing your friend." That's when all my hurt, care, and feelings poured out to the Lord. I cried and told Him how I felt. As I told the Lord about all these stuffed-down feelings, I felt His peace and love comfort me.

How many times have I said to myself, "If only someone would care, really care, how I feel…" But how can anyone know how you're feeling if you never tell them? My thinking was that God knows everything, so why should I have to tell Him? He knows already.

I decided that no one wanted to listen to me, that no one really cared how I was feeling. Once that becomes part of your thinking, I believe that it transfers over to how you think about the Father. You wonder to yourself, "Does He want to listen to me? Does He care?" Oh my. That is such a lie from the enemy! Of course God listens and cares. In His Word, He tells us that not only does He care for us, but He watches over us. He cares for us affectionately. Psalm 55:16–17 tells us that He will hear our voice. In writing the psalms, David knew that he could give his concerns and feelings to the Lord continuously, day and night. He is such an example for us when it comes to pouring out our hearts to the Lord.

One day a friend poured out his heart to me and shared about how he had struggled as a youngster going to boarding school. As he shared, tears poured out of my eyes. I thought of my brother and how he must have hurt going to the convent as a young boy. I couldn't remember anything from that time in my life. All I remembered was walking up steps and seeing two big doors shut. I remembered crying, because I wanted my brother. I wanted to go with him. Aside from that, this period of my life was completely closed to me.

I believe the pain of my brother being gone caused me to shut out all my feelings. I closed my heart. I was so concerned for my brother that I totally ignored my feelings. Wanting him to come home was too much for me to deal with as a little girl. My parents were probably struggling with their own emotions, and they did the best they could to explain to me what was happening, but I was devastated. I just wanted to save my brother.

I can't say for sure, because I don't remember thinking it at the time, but I may have wondered if nobody cared about me, not even God.

When I opened my heart, I knew that I needed to deal with this area of my life and heart. I realized I had so much unforgiveness buried deep toward the church, my parents, and God. I had to forgive them for what I had lost and the affects they'd had on my life. Some of the exposed emotions included loneliness, abandonment, fear, anger, terror, insecurity, worry, guilt, hopelessness, heartbrokenness, unhappiness, and sadness.

I was able to give all these emotions to the Father and He healed my broken heart. He gave me a vision of Him holding me in his arms with my head on his shoulder while standing on steps that looked like church steps. A few weeks later, I was given a picture of Jesus holding a little girl in His arms, and she had her head on His shoulder. What a beautiful confirmation! How He cares for us.

A few weeks later, I thought, *I don't feel that loneliness deep down anymore. Many of my fears are gone, especially the fear of being abandoned.* I don't have the words to explain the new sense of peace that came into my heart. Sometimes I still get lonely, but it's not the fear-gripping loneliness I used to have.

Casting the whole of your care [all your anxieties, all your worries, all your concerns, once and for all] on Him, for He cares for you affectionately and cares about you watchfully.
—1 Peter 5:7, AMPC

As for me, I will call upon God, and the Lord will save me. Evening and morning and at noon will I utter my complaint and moan and sigh, and He will hear my voice… Cast your burden on the Lord [releasing the weight of it] and He will sustain you; He will never allow the [consistently] righteous to be moved (made to slip, fall, or fail).
—Psalm 55:16–17, 22, AMPC

In our society, we have become so used to saying we're fine that I sometimes wonder if we can be honest about how we feel. I wonder how much of this type of thinking has become so much a part of our thinking that we've become accustomed to believing we actually are fine. I have to laugh. I wonder how often our fine really means Feeling Intense Negative Emotions.

But we find it necessary to say, "I'm fine. I'm great. I'm wonderful." How often have we been told that we're just complaining if we express our feelings? How often have we heard someone say, "Quit complaining. No one wants to hear your troubles. Keep your chin up. Life isn't that bad. Keep chugging away. Complaining does no good anyway"? Sometimes worry, care, and concern becomes confidential, so of course you don't want to talk about it to everyone. So it just seems easier to say that you're fine.

For me, this so easily transferred over to how I dealt with the Father. Is this how God wants us to deal with our feelings, cares, and concerns? How does God want us to deal with them? What does God have to say about talking to Him about our cares, troubles, and worries?

I started to wonder, if it's so wrong to talk about our cares, troubles, burdens, and complaints, why does God in His Word tell us to give Him our cares? God tells us more than once in the Word to cast our concerns on Him. Our Father knows what we really need as His children. He knew we would need to know we had a Father who listens and cares about our feelings, that we aren't alone, that we are so important to the Father that He wants to know all our concerns and care for us.

I've learned that ignoring my cares and emotions—to protect myself, not trusting them to God—is the same as stuffing them down. They don't go away. But He cares. He wants us to talk to Him about everything. He wants to be our friend. He sent us the Holy Spirit to be our Helper, Counsellor, and Healer.

It doesn't help to ignore our cares and stuff them down. We have to do something about them, and the Word very clearly tells us what to do: cast your burdens on Him and He will sustain you. I'm convinced that if we don't cast our cares and concerns onto the Lord, or give it to Him or talk about it, we're saying, "I can handle this on my own. I can forget about it and deal with it. I don't need you." When I used to say this, I didn't mean that I didn't need the Lord, but my actions spoke differently.

Our heavenly Father gives us free will to take this approach of handling things on our own. It isn't His perfect choice for us. He so much wants to care for us, affectionately. We need to allow the Father to care by opening up to Him. How wonderful it is to know we don't have to handle our cares and concerns on our own. We have a heavenly Father who's just waiting for us to give him our cares and concerns. As soon as we cast our cares upon Him, He is there to help.

In Psalm 55, the psalmist calls upon the Lord all day long with his complaints. We can fellowship with the Lord all day, telling Him about our financial worries, about our children, about our health, about our marriages, etc.

After I learned the scripture about casting our cares upon the Lord, I was able to start doing that. But I missed the part of the scripture that says we are to cast *all* of our cares on Him. I gave God a particular situation, but I still didn't cast my feelings. I could cast what was happening around me, but there was more.

He cares about your heart. You can say, "Lord, I feel rejected. I feel lonely. I feel abandoned. I'm scared and fearful." Or you can even say, "Lord, I'm feeling so hurt. I'm angry. I don't even know what I'm feeling. Can you help me, Lord?"

Some days I would say, "Oh Lord, I know this is just a little thing, but I need help with this. It really bothers me." Then I would feel guilty and add, "Oh Lord, I'm bothering you with such little things." But the truth is that nothing is too small to talk to Jesus about. You are not a bother to the Lord.

If my children want help with something or tell me about a problem they're having, I don't think, *Why are they bothering me?* I may not be able to fix their problem, but I can show them that I care and love them and am concerned for them. This is how Jesus must think about us. He wants us to know we can trust Him with everything and talk to him about everything.

I use my children as an example because we're God's children. I want my children to feel free to come to me with their concerns and about what's happening in their lives. It hurts when they don't. I'm sure God feels the same way. He wants us, His children, to come to Him with all our cares.

One year I decided to cast my cares on the Lord by making a burden box. I was at a conference and the speaker had a box into which we were to put our burdens. We were supposed to leave them there. What a great idea! So I made a burden box at home. I would write whatever care or concern I had and then put it in the box. When that care would come to my mind again, I'd remind myself that I had placed it in the burden box. Now it was the Lord's to take care of and I couldn't do anything about it. This helped me remember to give my cares to the Lord and not take them back.

How easy it is to say "Lord, I ask you to help…" but then two minutes later start worrying about it again. So many times, we have no control over our concerns. We can ask the Lord what to pray and how to pray and be comforted that He cares—but we need to go the Lord.

You may ask, what's the difference between putting your cares in a burden box and just not dealing with them? When I didn't cast them to the Lord, I stuffed them down with all the emotional baggage they carried. By giving my cares to the Lord, I was admitting my need for Him to come alongside me and help me. I was giving Him permission to work with me, to be my comfort, my counsellor, my ever-present help.

Remember, God gives us the free will to do what we want and to handle everything our own way, but He so wants us to know that He's there for us as soon as we call for help. If I was to make a burden box now, I would put my feelings in the box, not just the situation. He cares and is just waiting for us to call on Him for help.

I wonder what I was really thinking when I asked, "God, don't you care?" Perhaps I really meant, "I don't think He cares how I feel." Of course He did, but I just didn't know how I was feeling. It was necessary to acknowledge how I was feeling so I could release that to Him.

How easy it is to be tempted to think that God doesn't care when things in our lives are hard or not going our way. The enemy so wants us to believe our heavenly Father isn't a caring Father. It's such a huge lie. Or perhaps we think that He does care, but that He doesn't care about us. This thinking is contrary to the Word and character of God.

There is such great freedom in knowing the Word and understanding the character of our caring Father. We can be assured that as we give Him our cares and feelings, we can trust Him to watch over us. We can trust Him to do what is best for us. We are not alone.

The Lie:
I have to suck it up. I need to be strong. God
doesn't want to hear about how I feel.

The Truth:
God cares affectionately for me and I can give
Him all my cares and emotions.

The journey continues as I look to the Father and trust Him with my cares and emotions—all my emotions—because that's how He created me: with emotions. I am His child and He is my loving, caring Father.

CHAPTER EIGHT

Look to God
to Know His
Character

How does a child form their views of God?
This is a huge topic.
How did you form your views of God?
When did you learn about God?
Who taught you about God?
Have your perceptions changed?
What do you use to teach you about the Father?

Many hindrances can prevent us from recognizing the love of God in our hearts. Our hearts can be damaged throughout our lives, causing us to perceive the Lord through damaged hearts. I don't want to deal with all the ways in which we can get a misconception of the nature and love of God. Instead I'd like to talk about using people's behaviour as a benchmark to form our view of God.

I was blessed to be born into a family that knew about God. Going to church was very important to us. When I was young, I somehow thought clergy was the closest to being like God. There's a big danger in looking at Christians and clergy and using their actions to form your idea of the nature of God. People sometimes forget that Christians are human, that clergy are human and make mistakes. We all sin and fall short.

Since all have sinned and are falling short of the honor and glory which God bestows and receives.
—Romans 3:23, AMPC

When I was young, I was told that the clergy represented God, that they speak for Him. While there is truth to these statements, I perceived it to mean that what the clergy said and did was directly correlated to the character of God.

When I was very young, four or five, I was yelled at in church. It was devastating for me. I thought God was mad at me, that He was very disappointed in me. Therefore, I felt that I was a disappointment to Him. I had strived to be very well-behaved and thought I had been doing good.

I had a little friend who didn't have any money to give in the collection, so I brought my savings—a little purse of change—to give him some money so he could give to the church, too. The minister saw this and thought I was talking and playing with money in church. For that, I was disciplined. He told me very sternly, in front of everyone, that I was not at church to play with money and talk.

My young mind concluded that I was very naughty and God must be angry with me. Fear entered in and I formed the conclusion that I was to make sure I never did anything wrong again. If I did, I most certainly wouldn't be treated with love. Sometimes I ask myself why I was scared to do something wrong and get scolded by God.

Not long after, we had a new minister who was very kind and loving. I experienced kindness from him, but I still knew the necessity of behaving in church. My life was based on fear. I was scared to do anything wrong, thinking that I was protecting myself from God being mad at me. This was a big deception, a lie.

When I was a young adult, still trying to do the right thing and bring my children to church, my young son made lots of noise during the church service because he wanted to leave. The minister asked me to leave because my son was being so noisy. Because of my deep desire to love God and do what was right, I continued going to church. I forgave as best I could and stuffed down my feelings. I experienced other incidents that hurt my heart and added questions about God in my mind.

Reading the Word and studying the character of God helped me to realize who God was. My *mind* could justify forgiving the people who had hurt me, but my *heart* held on to the hurt. God knew I had a broken heart. He knew I needed healing. The Holy Spirit taught me about the heart and the importance of having a healed heart.

Scripture promises us that He heals the brokenhearted and sets the captive free. I needed to be set free and I needed my heart healed. I'm so thankful that by the love and healing of God, I was set free from the pain and hurt. Satan tried to deceive me, but the Holy Spirit nudged me along until I experienced healing and forgiveness and could embrace the Father's love in my soul and spirit.

Since I've been a Christian, I know that I've hurt people unintentionally. I don't want them to look at me and think, *That's the nature and character of God.* I also don't want to base any of my perceptions of the Father on what other people do. I've so often heard people say, "If that's what God is like, I don't want any part of it. They are looking at the people and thinking that they represent God. *Never* look at people and judge the loving character of God by their actions. Ask God to give you a revelation of His character and love. Allow the love of God to heal all those areas in your life where you have been hurt by God's people.

Take a minute and ask yourself, "What do I think the character of God is like? Has anyone in godly authority hurt me? Where have I looked at Christians and judged Jesus by them? Where have I been hurt or disillusioned by church, by clergy, by leaders? Have I allowed satan in any way to twist the truth of who God is by looking at others?"

As you read the below scriptures, ask the Holy Spirit to reveal where your mind may have a distorted view of God. These are just a few of the many, many scriptures that reveal the character of God and how He treats us.

> *But God, who is rich in mercy, because of His great love with which He loved us, even when we were dead in trespasses, made us alive together with Christ (by grace you have been saved), and raised us up together, and made us sit together in the heavenly places in Christ Jesus...*
> —Ephesians 2:4–6, NKJV

> *For we also were once thoughtless and senseless, obstinate and disobedient, deluded and misled; [we too were once] slaves to all sorts of cravings and pleasures, wasting our days in malice and jealousy and envy, hateful (hated, detestable) and hating one another. But when the goodness and loving-kindness of God our Savior to man [as man] appeared, He saved us, not because of any works of righteousness that we had done, but because of His own pity and mercy, by [the] cleansing [bath] of the new birth (regeneration) and renewing of the Holy Spirit...*
> —Titus 3:3–5, AMPC

> *Your mercy, O Lord, is in the heavens; Your faithfulness reaches to the clouds. Your righteousness is like the great mountains; Your judgments are a great deep; O Lord, You*

preserve man and beast. How precious is Your lovingkind-ness, O God! Therefore the children of men put their trust under the shadow of Your wings… Oh, continue Your lov-ingkindness to those who know You…

—Psalm 36:5–7, 10, NKJV

And the Lord passed before him and proclaimed, "The Lord, the Lord God, merciful and gracious, longsuffering, and abounding in goodness and truth, keeping mercy for thou-sands, forgiving iniquity and transgression…"

—Exodus 34:6–7, NKJV

The Lord is gracious and full of compassion, slow to anger and great in mercy. The Lord is good to all, and His tender mercies are over all His works.

—Psalm 145:8–9, NKJV

So be merciful (sympathetic, tender, responsive, and compas-sionate) even as your Father is [all these].

—Luke 6:36, AMPC

For we do not have a High Priest who cannot sympathize with our weaknesses, but was in all points tempted as we are, yet without sin. Let us therefore come boldly to the throne of grace, that we may obtain mercy and find grace to help in time of need.

—Hebrews 4:15–16, NKJV

He heals the brokenhearted and binds up their wounds.

—Psalm 147:3, NKJV

The Lord is near to those who have a broken heart, and saves such as have a contrite spirit.
—Psalm 34:18, NKJV

So many words describe our God. He heals the broken hearted. He is merciful, sympathetic, compassionate, full of grace, abounding in goodness, longsuffering, loving, kind, faithful, and righteous. He shows pity and is gracious, truthful, and loving. What a wonderful God we serve.

The Lie:
The clergy represents God and His nature. If you're Christian, you must represent God by doing nothing wrong so that people will know who God is.

The Truth:
Look only to God and His Word to know His nature.

The journey continues as the nature of the Father is revealed in my whole being—spirit, soul, and body. I allow the love of the Father to reach the depths of my heart so that I can seek Him with an open heart and receive His love. I need to ask myself, "Is this what the Father would tell me? Is this what He would say? Where is this thought really coming from?"

CHAPTER NINE

God
Approves

Does God approve of you?
Do you approve of yourself?

I t's one thing for me to believe that God has fearfully and
wonderfully made me, but believing that He approves of
me is a different story.

I felt that I had to be perfect to get God's approval, and
that led me on a rollercoaster ride. I so wanted God's approval.
Who doesn't want approval? I wanted to be a good person in
the eyes of the Lord. I wanted to please Him so that I could
get His approval, and the only way I could please Him was to
do everything right.

That's a pretty hard task to put on a person, whether
they're a child, teenager, or adult.

What did this roller coaster ride look like? What was it that
made me feel He approved? What made me feel disapproval?

In school, I tried very hard to be the perfect student. I
was obedient, I worked hard, and I felt so proud and validated
when I got high grades. Did you get high grades? What happens to the person who cannot do well in school and doesn't
get good grades? If I got a low grade, should that have meant I
wasn't satisfactory?

In my first year of university, I loved math. I had always been very good at math, but one day I got a grade of seven out of ten. I was so devastated that it made me feel like a failure. I dropped the course. That was a huge mistake, but my ability to feel good about myself was tied to my math skills. I guess that's the only way I can explain it. I was looking to grades for approval, not knowing that God already approved of me.

If I felt people approved of me and my performance met their standards, I felt good about myself and accepted by people and God.

But what happened when people didn't approve? I turned into a different person. The minute I felt disapproval, I got nervous, insecure, defensive, scared, and tormented in my mind. I did my best to put up a front to show people I was okay, but being around people was often difficult. My self-talk would turn negative: "They think I'm stupid. They think I don't know anything. They hate me even though I never did anything wrong. What can I do? Help me, Lord." Nothing took away that disapproving self-talk so I just smiled and pretended to be happy.

I could tell you story after story of my days of feeling disapproval, whether the disapproval was real or not. The more tormented I became, the more I craved approval. I wanted it so bad that I wasn't myself.

Then there was the other side. I had wonderful people in my life who gave me lots of encouraging, approving words. If I received encouraging words, it felt safe to be me. I called myself a chameleon, acting and reacting according to the environment I was in to gain approval.

God started to deal with me in this area of my life. As I sought prayer and inner healing, the very hurtful feelings of disapproval were dealt with. I repented, forgave, and was healed. My mind still struggled in certain situations, but this happened less and less.

Have you ever wanted to be free from something, but it just stayed there, clinging on? Have you ever felt good but then got a look for supposedly saying the wrong thing, which set off the feelings of disapproval in your head all over again? Perhaps you said to yourself, "If people don't approve of me, I must be doing something wrong. Therefore God must disapprove of me, because if I was godly enough, people would approve."

Such lies. Pure lies.

One day in Bible study, the leader looked at me and said, "God approves of you." I thought, *Oh really?* She said it over and over: "God approves of you. The God of the universe approves of *you.*"

A few weeks later, she said again, "God approves of you. He is the King and no king would put his seal upon anything unless he approved." Read with me what the leader said next:

> *[He has also appropriated and acknowledged us as His by] putting His seal upon us and giving us His [Holy] Spirit in our hearts as the security deposit and guarantee [of the fulfillment of His promise].*
>
> —2 Corinthians 1:22, AMPC

Then she asked me, "Do you believe you have the Holy Spirit in you? If you do, you have His seal upon you. Isn't it great to know that He approves of us and puts His seal on us?" I had to agree.

Do I still struggle in situations with feeling disapproval? Of course, but not for long. I use the Word to remind myself that God approves. I fight the lies of the enemy with the truth.

You will never get approval from all men. The approval of man doesn't equate to the approval of God. Jesus walked on the Earth and received much disapproval. What a lie it is to believe that all people will approve of you. Who should I go to for the source of approval? My Father in heaven. It doesn't matter what others think of me; God approves.

Max Lucado's book, *You Are Special*, there's a group of people, the Wemmecks, who gave out dots for things that were wrong with people and stars for things that were right with them. When I first read the book, my focus was on the dots. A character named Punchinello always got dots, never any stars—until he met Lucia, who had neither dots nor stars. Lucia then brought Punchinello to Eli the Maker; Eli was her maker, and she visited him every day. Once Punchinello started visiting Eli, the dots began to fall off him.[8]

One day, it struck me that Lucia didn't have any stars sticking to her either. From within me, I felt the Holy Spirit say, "Stars can be just as dangerous as dots." Some people are always looking for stars and learning how to get them. In the story, though, Lucia didn't need any stars, because her maker, Eli, gave her all the approval she needed. Because of her relationship with Eli, even when the dots came, they never stuck to her.

What a great analogy this is of our Father. We don't need to let other people's disapproval stick to us. When we go to the Lord, He gives us all the love and approval we need. We can give Him all the disapproval we feel and He'll take it all away.

What is more important? To know what God says about you or to get stars of approval from others? What does the Holy Spirit say about us? Who is our maker and what does He say about us?

---

8   Max Lucado, *You Are Special* (Wheaton, IL: Crossway Books, 1997).

Scripture after scripture, the Word tells us who we are when Christ lives in us. Whose report are you going to believe? Are you going to let dots stick to you? How about stars?

We all need encouragement, and to encourage one another, but let God the Father be the one to give you your approval. He approves of you!

When you come from a position of feeling approved of, you see the world from a different perspective. This doesn't necessarily mean that God approves of everything you do, but He approves of the person He created and He's here to help you grow and change.

He made me and He knows me inside and out. He knows everything about me and He's there to walk with me each moment. More than that, His love motivates me to be all that I am. I don't have to strive for approval and try to make myself someone I was never meant to be.

It's sad how much of my life I spent trying to do things just to get approval, to be accepted by others. Our whole world is full of people looking for approval and waiting to be told they are satisfactory, and all the while the King of Kings is just waiting to let us know that He loves us and accepts us.

When we receive a revelation of how great the Father's love is for us, and when we live out of His love, because His Son lives in us, we will stop looking for approval. There will be no need, because *"[t]here is not fear in love; but perfect love casts out fear, because fear involves torment"* (1 John 4:18, NKJV). There's no need to fear disapproval.

The Lie:
I've got to prove myself, be perfect, and get others
approval in order for God to approve of me.

The Truth:
God approves of me because He created
me and loves me.

The journey continues as I walk in the Father's approval, and as I allow the revelation of who He created me to be, my true identity. Living in the truth causes me to run quickly to my Father when I feel disapproval.

CHAPTER TEN

Be Transformed
in the Mind and
Know the Truth
in the Heart

Is the Lord concerned about your heart?
Are your thoughts more important than your heart?
Can you use your intellect and think in your own way?
Does your heart have any control of you?
How do you know what's in your heart?
What does the Word say about the heart?

Throughout the book, I've written about how I was changed in my mind and heart, and how it's been a journey and a process. I wasn't the sort of person who had a sudden transformation. I walked step by step as the Lord led me.

The Bible was my source of truth. It showed me the way to go, and how to live.

> *Do not be conformed to this world (this age), [fashioned after and adapted to its external, superficial customs], but be transformed (changed) by the [entire] renewal of your mind [by its new ideals and its new attitude], so that you may prove [for yourselves] what is the good and acceptable and perfect will of God, even the thing which is good and acceptable and perfect [in His sight for you].*
>
> —Romans 12:2, AMPC

Reading the Word of God transformed my mind in many ways. When I would read the Word, it was like a verse would pop off the page. When the Word stood out to me, I knew there was something there for me to learn. I would pause, meditate, and ask the Lord what revelation He wanted me to understand. The Lord wanted to teach me at that moment—not just in my mind, but in my heart. I needed a revelation of the truth so that I could see with the new eyes of my heart. Knowing something in my head has never changed me, but knowing something and getting a revelation in my heart is transformative.

I've learned several truths from parents, teachers, friends, grandparents, church leaders, books, and the media. How could I know that what they taught about Christ and God was correct? I had so many ideas in my head that I didn't know what was truth from the Word and what wasn't. Reading the Word helped me to look at what I was taught and test it with the Word.

Throughout my years of reading the Word, I have continued learning and having my mind be renewed with new revelation and truth. When reading, the Holy Spirit has shown me what's in my heart, not just what I believe in my mind.

For the Word that God speaks is alive and full of power [making it active, operative, energizing, and effective]; it is sharper than any two-edged sword, penetrating to the dividing line of the breath of life (soul) and [the immortal] spirit, and of joints and marrow [of the deepest parts of our nature], exposing and sifting and analysing and judging the very thoughts and purposes of the heart.

—Hebrews 4:12, AMPC (emphasis added)

When the scripture refer to your heart, what do they really mean? Is the Lord concerned about your heart? Are our thoughts more important than our heart? Can we just know and use our intellect and think our own way? Does our heart have any control of us? How do we know what's in our heart? What does the Word say about the heart?

When the Word of God renewed my mind, I started learning many truths. Just like with the love of God, I knew the words of scripture in my head, but it was necessary to know them in my heart. With every truth I learned, I had to allow that truth to get into my heart.

How could I move the truth to my heart? How could I walk out the truths I was learning?

Knowing the truth in your head and living the truth in your whole being, I realized, are not the same. When you know a truth in your head, you can quote the scripture, but you don't act on it. It hasn't become part of your life.

I wanted to change and become more Christ-like, drawing closer to the Lord. I also wanted the Holy Spirit to work in my life.

I read the Word, and with my intellect I knew what it said. I was trying to live the Word by transforming my intellect. I was on a rollercoaster ride. I knew I was learning the Word, but I hadn't realized the extent to which my mind still allowed in thoughts that didn't agree with the Word of God. If my thoughts weren't in agreement with the truth of God, they were lies.

As I sat back and reflected, I said, "Yes, I have believed so many lies." Lies from the enemy are very deceptive. I often didn't even realize I was believing a lie. No one knows the lies that are bombarding them in their inner dialogue. No one knows the truths that pass through their mind, either. It's between you and God.

I frequently felt like I was being tortured in my mind. My mind would whip me. Sometimes I could fight back and get that wrong thought out of my head. Other times I was bombarded with self-condemning thoughts of regret, wrongs, and torment. I would smile to myself and continue to say that everything was fine.

I've shared some of these tormenting thoughts, as well as how I've learned to expose the lies and use the Word of God to counteract them. A lie starts with a thought, and satan likes to plant those little thoughts in your mind. He did that in the Garden of Eden by saying to Eve, "Did God really say that?" Satan put a seed of doubt in Eve's thoughts. Imagine Adam and Eve walking and talking with God in the garden. They knew Him. If satan could so easily deceive Eve, he is out to deceive anyone he can.

> Now the serpent was more cunning than any beast of the field which the Lord God had made. And he said to the woman, "Has God indeed said, 'You shall not eat of every tree of the garden'?"
> And the woman said to the serpent, "We may eat the fruit of the trees of the garden; but of the fruit of the tree which is in the midst of the garden, God has said, 'You shall not eat it, nor shall you touch it, lest you die.'"
> Then the serpent said to the woman, "You will not surely die. For God knows that in the day you eat of it your eyes will be opened, and you will be like God, knowing good and evil."
>
> —Genesis 3:1–5, NKJV

> The thief comes only in order to steal and kill and destroy. I came that they may have and enjoy life, and have it in abundance (to the full, till it overflows).
>
> —John 10:10, AMPC

82

God gave Adam and Eve abundant life. They knew Him in their heart, they knew of His love, and they spent time talking with Him. They were still deceived when they let a thought remain in their mind and didn't get rid of it with the truth of God.

How did they get deceived? Satan planted thoughts in their minds that seemed right. How do you let satan in? What lies are you believing? Does your inner dialogue sound the same as the Word that the Lord gives you?

Jesus came so that we could have abundant life. He told us in John 14:6 that He is the way, the truth, and the life. Our loving heavenly Father sent Jesus to destroy the works of the enemy.

The more the truth is revealed to us, the easier it is to combat the lies. God knew that my desire was to believe the truth, not a lie. I so wanted to walk in truth. I so wanted to please Him. I often sit back in awe of how loving the Father is and how He knows exactly what we need.

When I sit back and reflect on my life, I sometimes ask, "Why didn't I just believe the truth? Why did I believe lies? Why did it take me so long?" I've found that dwelling on these whys hasn't been helpful. Moving on to the truth has been. The truth is where the heart comes in. The Word of God will judge the very thoughts and purposes of the heart.

> *For the Word that God speaks is alive and full of power [making it active, operative, energizing, and effective]; it is sharper than any two-edged sword, penetrating to the dividing line of the breath of life (soul) and [the immortal] spirit, and of joints and marrow [of the deepest parts of our nature],* exposing and sifting and analyzing *and judging the very thoughts and purposes of the heart.*
> —Hebrews 4:12, AMPC (emphasis added)

I made the choice to ask the Father for a revelation about what was buried deep inside—the pain and hurt which formed my thinking. What's in your heart affects you. I needed to forgive, I needed to expose the lies, I needed to be healed, I needed to know the truth.

Some truths took a long time to get into my heart. As I read the Word, heard preaching of the Word, and attended Bible studies, my heart was exposed. God allowed me to see my heart. My mind was being renewed and my heart was being healed.

> *Every Scripture is God-breathed (given by His inspiration) and profitable for instruction, for reproof and conviction of sin, for correction of error and discipline in obedience, [and] for training in righteousness (in holy living, in conformity to God's will in thought, purpose, and action), So that the man of God may be complete and proficient, well fitted and thoroughly equipped for every good work.*
> —2 Timothy 3:16–17, AMPC

> *But be doers of the Word [obey the message], and not merely listeners to it, betraying yourselves [into deception by reasoning contrary to the Truth].*
> —James 1:22, AMPC (emphasis added)

How easy it is to be deceived. At many points in my life, I had been positive I was obeying the truth, but I often betrayed myself and believed otherwise by listening to my own reasoning.

Satan was very successful at deceiving Eve, and he also tried to tempt Jesus with his twisted truth. When Jesus was fasting in the wilderness, satan came and tempted Him, but

Jesus used the Word of God to combat satan's lies (Matthew 4:1–11).

In what ways does your mind allow you to use reasoning instead of the truth? Aren't we taught to reason? To analyze? Jesus didn't try to reason. He knew the truth, stated the truth, and didn't let satan tempt him.

My life wasn't transformed by reasoning in my mind. It was a process. Being transformed by the renewing of my mind came when God gave me revelations in my heart—one revelation at a time. He used a variety of ways to help me to know the truth in my heart, and transformation came once I was healed. I often needed my hurts to be healed, as well as a touch of God's love before my mind was transformed. Every time the Lord brought to my attention the hurts that had been stuffed down in my heart, I discovered that I had unforgiveness attached there. Hurt and unforgiveness seemed to go together.

Sometimes I just needed the revelation truth to be revealed so that I could believe what I was reading in the Word. I would ask God to help me get it. Then, like a lightbulb being turned on, I would say, "I really get this now. I get this in my heart, not just in my head." I believed what I was reading in the Word and walked in what I believed. This is revelation knowledge.

Transformation also came when I heard testimonies similar to situations in my own life and related to them. These testimonies often touched my heart. I saw how people would forgive, how they would love, how God would heal their bodies and hearts and emotions. This encouraged me because I knew that what God could do for someone else, He could do for me.

All the ways of a man are pure in his own eyes, but the Lord weighs the spirits (the thoughts and intents of the heart).
—Proverbs 16:2, AMPC

My mind could learn and reason the Word of God, but my heart had to be right for true transformation to occur. God had to reveal what was in my heart. As I said, I couldn't fully believe that God loved me until my heart was healed.

When a person has the truth revealed in his heart and his mind is transformed, he has a choice whether to keep the truth. It's a continual choice—to choose the truth over a lie. We have to choose to set our minds on things above. Satan waits for times when we're weak to place thoughts in our minds. These are lies to tempt us or to allow an offense to snare our hearts.

And set your minds and keep them set on what is above (the higher things), not on the things that are on the earth.
—Colossians 3:2, AMPC

Do not be conformed to this world (this age), [fashioned after and adapted to its external, superficial customs], but be transformed (changed) by the [entire] renewal of your mind [by its new ideals and its new attitude], so that you may prove [for yourselves] what is the good and acceptable and perfect will of God, even the thing which is good and acceptable and perfect [in His sight for you].
—Romans 12:2, AMPC

Your word have I laid up in my heart, that I might not sin against You.
—Psalm 119:11, AMPC

God wants us to be transformed in our minds, and to let our hearts store His Word.

Blessed (happy, fortunate, to be envied) are they who keep His testimonies, and who seek, inquire for and of Him and crave Him with the whole heart.

—Psalm 119:2, AMPC

Our minds can learn and be transformed, but we need to seek the Lord with all our hearts.

Then you will seek Me, inquire for, and require Me [as a vital necessity] and find Me when you search for Me with all your heart.

—Jeremiah 29:13, AMPC

God promises that if we seek Him with our heart, we will find Him.

Create in me a clean heart, O God, and renew a right, persevering, and steadfast spirit within me.

—Psalm 51:10, AMPC

As we seek the Lord and ask Him to expose and clean our hearts, He will show us how to experience abundant life.

For the Lord sees not as man sees; for man looks on the outward appearance, but the Lord looks on the heart.

—1 Samuel 16:7, AMPC

God sees our hearts, so there's no use trying to hide what's in there. God sees it all and wants to be there for us.

But from there you will seek the Lord your God, and you will find Him if you seek Him with all your heart and with all your soul.

—Deuteronomy 4:29, NKJV

Seeking and finding the Lord requires us to seek Him with everything, all our hearts.

Therefore know this day, and consider it in your heart, that the Lord Himself is God in heaven above and on the earth beneath; there is no other.

—Deuteronomy 4:39, NKJV

God is telling us to know the truth in our hearts.

Oh, that they had such a heart in them that they would fear Me and always keep all My commandments, that it might be well with them and with their children forever!

—Deuteronomy 5:29, NKJV

…having their understanding darkened, being alienated from the life of God, because of the ignorance that is in them, because of the blindness of their heart.

—Ephesians 4:18, NKJV

We need to pray that God will remove the blindness from our hearts so that our understanding won't be darkened.

My little children, let us not love in word or in tongue, but in deed and in truth. And by this we know that we are of the truth, and shall assure our hearts before Him. For if our heart condemns us, God is greater than our heart, and knows all things. Beloved, if our heart does not condemn us, we have confidence toward God.

—1 John 3:18–21, NKJV

Therefore give to Your servant an understanding heart to judge Your people, that I may discern between good and evil.

—1 Kings 3:9, NKJV

But whatever comes out of the mouth comes from the heart, and this is what makes a man unclean and defiles [him].

—Matthew 15:18, AMPC

Listen to what's coming out of your mouth, or what's entering your thoughts. This is what's in your heart. Do not be deceived or condemned. As a person admits and deals with their heart issues, they can seek God with all their heart and abundant life will flow through them.

Paul prayed for the people under his care. This is what he prayed, and I use it as a prayer for everyone who reads this book:

[For I always pray to] the God of our Lord Jesus Christ, the Father of glory, that He may grant you a spirit of wisdom and revelation [of insight into mysteries and secrets] in the [deep and intimate] knowledge of Him, by having the eyes of your heart *flooded with light, so that you can know and understand the hope to which He has called you, and how rich is His glorious inheritance in the saints (His set-apart ones), and [so that you can know and understand] what is the immeasurable and unlimited and surpassing greatness of His power in and for us who believe, as demonstrated in the working of His mighty strength…*

—Ephesians 1:17–19, AMPC

(emphasis added)

The Lie:
We just need to know the truth with our
intellectual minds.

The Truth:
We need a revelation of the Word in our hearts (our
spirits) and in our minds so that we may be
transformed, healed, and delivered.

My exciting journey continues with the Father, with my
eyes being opened and new truths being revealed. My heart
has been healed by the one who was sent to heal the brokenhearted and set the captives free: Jesus.

Conclusion

I could write an entire book—and indeed, books have been written—about the subjects of each chapter in this book. I'm only writing about my experience of learning the truth of these topics, not giving in-depth teaching. I believe the Father has wanted me to look at my inner dialogue, my thoughts, and my heart.

As I wrote this book, it was difficult to separate chapter from chapter because the topics weren't separate from each other. They are all intertwined. The more my mind was renewed, the more I could accept God's love. The more God's love touched my heart, the more I could forgive. The more I accepted God's forgiveness, the more I could forgive others. The more I forgave others, the more my heart was healed. The more I let anger go in my heart, the more I felt freedom. The more my broken heart was healed, the more I loved myself and others. The more I loved myself and others, the more I could forgive. The more I could forgive, the more I experienced the loving kindness of God.

Growing and walking the life God has for me has involved all the aspects in this book, in no particular order. I have shared a few of the areas of my life where I was set free in the spirit of my mind and heart. It has been a journey and will continue to be a journey. My goal is to *"be constantly renewed in the spirit of your mind [having a fresh mental and spiritual attitude]"* (Ephesians 4:23, AMPC).

I've learned that I don't have to be the protector of my heart. The Father is there to protect both my mind and heart. I just have to allow Him.

> *Be anxious for nothing, but in everything by prayer and supplication with thanksgiving let your requests be made known to God. And the peace of God, which surpasses all comprehension, will guard your hearts and your minds in Christ Jesus.*
>
> —Philippians 4:6–7, NASB

Throughout my life, it has been easy to give the Father my prayers and requests. But I had forgotten the second part of the verse. I would do everything I could to guard my own heart. It didn't work for me. I came to realize that the Father wanted to guard my heart and my mind. I just had to let Him. I had to let go of being my own protector.

I'm so thankful to God the Father, Jesus, and the Holy Spirit for never giving up on me. They have gently taught me and directed me along the path with patience.

When thoughts are planted in my mind, I have a choice. I can stop the thoughts right when they come in and instead believe what I've been taught, or I can meditate on them and let them bring me down. I can ask, "Where is this thought coming from?" That's a good question to remember. Does the thought come from God? Does it sound like the truth in the scriptures? Is it something God would say?

> *But the Comforter (Counselor, Helper, Intercessor, Advocate, Strengthener, Standby), the Holy Spirit, Whom the Father*

will send in My name [in My place, to represent Me and act on My behalf], He will teach you all things. And He will cause you to recall (will remind you of, bring to your remembrance) everything I have told you. Peace I leave with you; My [own] peace I now give and bequeath to you. Not as the world gives do I give to you. Do not let your hearts be troubled, neither let them be afraid. [Stop allowing yourselves to be agitated and disturbed; and do not permit yourselves to be fearful and intimidated and cowardly and unsettled.]
—John 14:26–27, AMPC

If you live in Me [abide vitally united to Me] and My words remain in you and continue to live in your hearts, ask whatever you will, and it shall be done for you.
—John 15:7, AMPC

I've often been told that I am insecure. Yes, in the world it may have looked like I was insecure. I was unable to move past my insecurities using the world's methods. I look at the word insecure now and choose to turn it around: I am *secure in* Christ, secure in His love, secure in His forgiveness, secure in His care, secure in His comfort, and secure in the person He created me to be. My mind and heart choose to no longer allow insecurity to be part of my life. I choose to be secure in Him, my Father.

These are just a few of the big lies I began to overcome during this walk I call life. The enemy is a liar and he tries to tempt me with old thought patterns, especially when I'm tired and feeling weak. I'm so thankful that I have the Holy Spirit, my Helper, Advocate, and Counsellor who reminds me of the truth. I am so thankful to the Father, Son, and Holy Spirit, who have been with me in this journey. They will continue to be with me, strengthening me to *live in the truth* and leave the lies behind.

The lies I once believed and the truth I now live have changed my life. I no longer have a tormented mind. I no longer have thoughts racing and bombarding my head, battling to destroy my peace. I know how to deal with my feelings and allow my heart to be healed. Christ truly came to heal the brokenhearted and set the captives free. I was one of them.

In conclusion, I can only say that surrendering and letting the Father reveal Himself to me, and allowing Him to renew my heart, has been life-changing. Is my life perfect? No, not at all. I don't seek perfection. I seek to walk in the truth and be in the loving presence of the Father, walking the path He has set before me, knowing the Father and knowing His Word. He loves me, forgives me, approves of me, cares for me, gives me strength to forgive, reveals His loving character, and helps me manage my emotions.

That's the truth I believe and now live!

I am so thankful that I can walk this journey with the Father, His Son Jesus, and the Holy Spirit. It is an amazing journey.